ESTABLISHED

Achievement in Year 10 English

Jenny Thomas and Diane White

NELSON
CENGAGE Learning

Australia • Brazil • Japan • Korea • Mexico • Singapore • Spain • United Kingdom • United States

NELSON
CENGAGE Learning

Building On ... Achievment in Year 10 English ESTABLISHED
1st Edition
Jenny Thomas
Diane White

Text and cover deign: Book Design Ltd
Typesetter: Book Design Ltd
Production controller: Siew Han Ong
Reprint: Jess Lovell

Any URLs contained in this publication were checked for currency during the production process. Note, however, that the publisher cannot vouch for the ongoing currency of URLs.

Acknowledgements
Our grateful thanks to all past and present colleagues who have so generously shared their expertise, creativity and resources. English departments thrive on your collegiality.

The authors and publisher wish to thank the following people and organisations for permission to use the resources in this textbook. Every effort has been made to trace and acknowledge all copyright owners of material used in this book. In most cases this was successful and copyright is acknowledged as requested. However, if any infringement has occurred the publishers tender their apologies and invite the copyright holders to contact them.

Pages 4, 6, 9, 10 Cemetery Path courtesy Leo Rosten; pages 6, 8, 9 The Sea Horse and the Reef by Witi Ihimaera, courtesy of Pearson Education, NZ; pages 10/11 At the Bay courtesy of Katherine Mansfield; page 11 The Writer courtesy of Richard Wilbur; pages 14/15 speech courtesy of Adam Daniels; Page 18 Hello Sir by Robbie Williams courtesy of EMI Virgin Music Ltd; page 22 Making a Meal of it by Jan Corbett courtesy of The New Zealand Herald; page 25 Thunder and Lightning courtesy of James Kirkup; page 28 advertisement courtesy of Animals Asia Foundation; page 34 The Old Place courtesy of the Hone Tuwhare Estate; page 39 The Snake Pit courtesy of Sonya Bates; page 40 Writing My Own Pantoum by Horace J. Digby courtesy of Lexington Film, LLC; page 41 A Pantoum in the New Zealand Bush courtesy of Sean Joyce; page 42 Friendly Persuasion courtesy of David Hill; page 46 advertisement courtesy of Genesis Energy; page 48 My Father Began as a God courtesy of the family of the late Ian Mudie; page 52 advertisement courtesy of Aoraki Polytechnic; page 54 Thawing ice heats debate on sovereignty by Daniel Howden, courtesy of The Independent; page 58 August, Ohakune courtesy of the Lauris Edmond Literary Estate; page 60 Cemetary Path courtesy of Leonard Q. Ross; page 72 Red by Bonnie Isiah; page 72 Jaguar courtesy of D.J. Brindley; page 73 The Big Time courtesy of Owen Marshall; page 74 cartoon courtesy of Garrick Tremain.

istock photos: page 57 (beach) Duncan Babbage

© 2010 Cengage Learning Australia Pty Limited

For product information and technology assistance,
in Australia call **1300 790 853**;
in New Zealand call **0800 449 725**

For permission to use material from this text or product, please email **aust.permissions@cengage.com**

National Library of New Zealand Cataloguing-in-Publication Data
Thomas, Jenny.
Building on-- achievement in year 10 English : established / Jenny Thomas and Diane White.
ISBN 978-0-17019-595-9
1. English language—Rhetoric—Juvenile literature. 2. English language—Composition and exercises—Juvenile literature. [1. English language—Rhetoric. 2. English language—Composition and exercises.] I. White, Diane. II. Title.
808.042—dc 22

Cengage Learning Australia
Level 7, 80 Dorcas Street
South Melbourne, Victoria Australia 3205

Cengage Learning New Zealand
Unit 4B Rosedale Office Park
331 Rosedale Road, Albany, North Shore 0632, NZ

For learning solutions, visit **cengage.co.nz**

Printed in Australia by Ligare Pty Limited.
7 8 9 10 11 12 13 20 19 18 17 16

Contents

This section connects directly to the first chapter of the accompanying textbook *How to ... Achieve in Year 10 English*. You may like to use this to make your life easier.

Read the extract below from the short story *Cemetery Path* written by Leonard Q. Ross and complete the activities that follow.

> Ivan was a timid little man – so timid that the villagers called him 'Pigeon' or mocked him with the title 'Ivan the Terrible'. Every night Ivan stopped at a saloon on the edge of the village cemetery. Ivan never crossed the cemetery to get to his lonely shack on the other side. The path through the cemetery would save him many minutes but Ivan had never taken it – not even in the full light of the moon.
>
> Late one winter's night, when a bitter wind and snow beat against the saloon, the customers took up their familiar mockery of Ivan. His mild protests only fed their taunts, and they laughed when a young Cossack lieutenant flung a challenge at their quarry. 'You are a pigeon, Ivan. A rabbit. A coward. You'll walk around the cemetery in this dreadful cold, to get home, but you dare not cross the cemetery.'

1 Nouns

Highlight five examples of common/concrete nouns.
Highlight three examples of proper nouns.
Highlight one example of an abstract noun.

2 Pronouns

List the pronouns used in this extract. _____

3 Adjectives

List the adjectives used in this extract. _____

4 Verbs

List at least 10 verbs used in this extract. _____

5 Adverbs

Find one example of an adverb of time in this extract. _____

6 Conjunctions

List three conjunctions used in this extract. _____

7 Prepositions

List three prepositions used in this extract. _____

ISBN 9780170195959

The definite article (the) indicates one particular person or thing.

The indefinite article (a/an) indicates a single but not particular thing.

Complete the following sentences inserting the appropriate **article** in each of the spaces.

1 _____ best show I ever saw was about _____ guy who wanted to be _____ astronaut.

2 He wanted to go to _____ moon so he needed _____ spaceship.

3 In _____ show the guy was either _____ Kiwi or _____ Australian, I couldn't tell.

4 In _____ end he didn't get there, but he met _____ alien on _____ planet, Mars.

The word 'tense' comes from the Latin word meaning 'time'. It means the form of the verb that tells the time of the action.

Highlight the verb in each of the following sentences and then change it from present to **past tense**.

1 The vocalist sings really well.
2 The drummer plays very loudly.
3 The guitarist breaks lots of strings.

Highlight the verb in each of the following sentences and then change it from past to **future tense**.

4 The audience applauded loudly.
5 The stagehands watched from the wings.
6 The MC encouraged the crowd to dance.

Highlight the verb in each of the following sentences and then change it from future to **present tense**.

7 The music will sound extremely loud.
8 The crowd will sing along with the vocalist.
9 The venue will be dark and steamy.

A pronoun stands in place of a noun. A possessive pronoun shows ownership. E.g. That skateboard is *mine*.

Fill the gap with the appropriate **possessive pronoun**.

1 Here is the elephant's food. It is _____
2 There is the tigress's meat. It is _____
3 This is the home of the gorillas and the monkeys. It is _____
4 You can have the job of cleaning the enclosure. The job is _____
5 The zoo entry free pass is for me and you. It's _____

The reflexive pronoun is used to refer back to someone mentioned earlier in the sentence.

Fill the gap with the appropriate **reflexive pronoun**.

1 Millie and Mandy asked for new shoes for _____
2 I wanted some time by _____ to read my book
3 My sister and I went to the school show by _____
4 Joe thought he could be in the show by _____
5 You and your partner can learn to dance by _____
6 Joe and Jodie printed the invitations by _____

Read the extract from the short story *The Sea Horse and the Reef* written by Witi Ihimaera below and complete the activities that follow. Please note some verb tenses have been changed. See question 1.

> The reef is just outside the town where my family lives. That was a long time ago, when I am a boy, before I was coming to this southern city. It was where all our relations and friends go every weekend in summer to dive for kai moana. The reef is the home of much kai moana – paua, pipi, kina, mussels, pupu and many other shell fish. It is the home too of other fish like flounder and octopus. It will teem with life and food. It will give its bounty to us. It is good to us.
>
> And it is where the seahorse lives.

1 One of the main problems we see in the writing of Year 10 students is mixing tenses. This passage should be all in the past tense but we have mixed present, past and future tenses. Your task is to write the whole thing in past tense. To make it easier we have highlighted the verbs you need to check.

_____
_____
_____
_____
_____
_____
_____

2 Highlight three examples of the definite article.

3 Highlight two examples of possessive adjectives.

4 Highlight one example of a possessive pronoun.

Use a blue pen to punctuate the following extract from the Leonard Q Ross short story *Cemetery Path*. Remember: new speaker, new line (use a [to mark a new line).

> Ivan murmured The cemetery – it is nothing to cross Lieutenant I am not afraid The cemetery is nothing but earth The lieutenant cried A challenge, then Cross the cemetery tonight, now, and I'll give you five gold roubles – five gold roubles Perhaps it was the vodka Perhaps it was the temptation of the five gold roubles No one ever knew why Ivan moistening his lips, blurted All right, Lieutenant I'll cross the cemetery

Think of a colon as a pause but not as big a pause as a full stop. It has several uses:

- A colon introduces a list.
- A colon may introduce a quotation or direct speech.
- In play scripts a colon follows the speaker's name, so it introduces dialogue.
- A colon may separate two parts of a sentence if the second one tells more about the first one or is the opposite of it.
- A colon is used in expressing time in numbers, which is much simpler than using words.

ISBN 9780170195959

Place a **colon** in the right place in each of the following sentences:

1   John ate his dinner two lamb chops, a mountain of mashed potato and three peas.

2   Ashley is great at sports he plays badminton, tennis, soccer and golf.

3   It's 1144 exactly.

4   Stephen asked politely 'Would you like fries with that?'

Semicolons

A semicolon marks a pause less than a full stop, but more than a comma. It can show connection between two distinct parts of a sentence. Semicolons are also used to separate items in a list where commas are already used.

Place a **semicolon** in the right place in each of the following sentences:

1   A winter's day is all freezing fingers and toes but it's all fires and warm toast, too.

2   That afternoon I ate six pink fluffy sticky marshmallows seven jellybeans all different colours a small packet of MandMs belonging to my sister and half a packet of biscuits.

3   Julia left a message on the answer phone she forgot to leave her name unfortunately.

Parentheses (brackets)

Parenthesis means one of a pair of curved signs (,) used to enclose an additional inserted word or comment and distinguish it from the sentence in which it is found.

Each sentence has additional information that could be enclosed in brackets. Place a set of **brackets** in the right place:

1   Marama stepped onto the plane her sister was right behind her and took a deep breath.

2   As the plane's engines roared a sound that inspires fear in many a traveller Marama gripped her sister's hand.

3   'It's OK,' said Mieke feeling slightly anxious herself 'it's only a few moments then we're up!'

Hyphen

A hyphen (-) is used to link parts of a compound word.

Place **hyphens** where they are required in compound words found in the following sentences:

1   Amy spoke to her sister in law on the phone.

2   The enormous ship was a man of war.

3   I caught the trans alpine train last week.

4   Alan is an anti nuclear protester.

5   The rock group is re forming.

Dash

The dash line (–) is slightly longer than the hyphen line. It separates parts of a sentence and forces us to pause. It can be used to:

- **create a dramatic pause**

- **mark a sudden turn in the thought of a sentence**

- **mark an unexpected ending.**

These sentences could use a **dash** (or two). Put them in the correct place(s).

1   I rang up Steve he's my best friend to ask for his advice.

2   Lucy leapt from the windowsill she landed unhurt on the lawn.

3   He waited; he waited a little longer then left abruptly.

A bullet point is a large dot (or other mark) to highlight items in a printed list.

Simplify this rambling phone message from Mum into a written **bulleted list** to take to the supermarket.

'Joe, can you go to the supermarket for me, please and get some toilet rolls, the ones with seashells on them; a couple of tins of baked beans, the ones without anything else in them; two loaves of bread, you choose a white and a brown; a small tub of butter, not the one that's half margarine; some frozen peas, I don't like the baby ones and a litre of milk, the sort that's got extra calcium in it. OK? Thanks.'

Read this passage from Witi Ihimaera's short story *The Seahorse and the Reef* and explain why each numbered punctuation mark has been used: NB: Witi Ihimaera punctuates speech in an unusual way.

At that time, our family lived in a small wooden house on the fringe of the industrial area. On a Sunday, my father would watch out the window and see our relations passing by on their old trucks and cars or bikes with their sugarbags and nets, their flippers and goggles, shouting and waving on their way to the reef. They came from the pa – 1 in those days it was not surrounded by expanding suburbia – 1 and they would sing out to Dad: 2

- Hey, Rongo! Come on! Good day for kai moana today!

Dad would sigh and start to moan and fidget. The lunch dishes had to be washed, the lawn had to be cut, my mother probably would want him to do other things round the house …3. Aue.

But after a while, a gleam would come into his eyes.

- 4 Hey, Huia! he would shout to Mum. Those kina are calling out loud to me today! 5

- So are the dishes, she would answer.

1 _____

2 _____

3 _____

4 _____

5 _____

ISBN 9780170195959

Let's check that you can identify these types of sentences. Read the extract from the short story *Cemetery Path* written by Leonard Q. Ross below and complete the activity that follows:

> 1 He recognised the large tomb. 2 No one could miss that large edifice. 3 Ivan must have sobbed – although that was drowned in the wind. 4 Ivan kneeled, cold and terrified, and in a frenzy of fear drove the saber into the hard ground. 5 It was hard to do, but he beat it down into the hard earth with his fist, down to the very hilt. 6 It was done! 7 The cemetery ... the challenge ... five roubles ... five gold roubles!

Identify the following in the above passage.
- three simple sentences   _____   _____   _____
- two compound sentences   _____   _____
- one complex sentence   _____
- one minor sentence   _____

Word order is very important in English.

Rearrange these sentences to make them make sense by putting the **subject** before the **verb**.

1 great match it was a _____

2 played well the team _____

3 scored six goals were _____

An active verb expresses action. A passive verb expresses the receiving of action.

Turn all of the following sentences, which use an active verb, into ones that use a **passive verb**. The first one has been done for you as an example.

1 *Active verb*: David **ate** a huge lunch. *Passive verb*: A huge lunch **was eaten** by David.

2 *Active verb*: Rob **kicked** three penalties. *Passive verb*:

_____

3 *Active verb*: A threatening black cloud **covered** the sky. *Passive verb*:

_____

4 *Active verb*: Seven girls **make up** a netball team. *Passive verb*:

_____

5 *Active verb*: Jill **is cooking** lunch today. *Passive verb*:

_____

1 If we asked you to find an example of a piece of writing that uses passive verbs it would be difficult because often the best writing uses active verbs. In this extract you will see a sentence using the passive voice alongside sentences using the active voice. Can you tell the difference? Highlight an example of each.

> The rock surrounding the pool was fringed with long waving seaweed. Small transparent fish swam among the waving leaves and little crabs scurried across the dark floor. The many pupu glided calmly along the sides of the pool. Once, a starfish inched its way into a dark crack.

2 Circle the subject of each of the above sentences.

Read this extract from the short story *Cemetery Path* written by Leonard Q. Ross below and complete the activities that follow:

> The wind howled around Ivan as he closed the door of the saloon behind him. The cold was as sharp as a butcher's knife. He buttoned his long coat and crossed the road. He could hear the lieutenant's voice, louder than the rest, calling after him, 'Five gold roubles, little pigeon! Five roubles – if you live!'
>
> Ivan strode to the cemetery gates, and hesitated, and pushed the gate open.
>
> He walked fast. 'Earth, it's just earth … like any other earth.' But the darkness was a massive dread. 'Five gold roubles …' The wind was savage and the saber was like ice in his hands. Ivan shivered under the long, thick coat and broke into a limping run.
>
> He recognised the large tomb. No one could miss that large edifice. Ivan must have sobbed – but that was drowned in the wind. And Ivan kneeled, cold and terrified, and in a frenzy of fear drove the saber into the hard ground. It was hard to do, but he beat it down into the hard earth with his fist, down to the very hilt. It was done! The cemetery … the challenge … five roubles … five gold roubles!

Highlight one example of each of these in the passage:

1 simile
2 metaphor
3 personification
4 alliteration
5 onomatopoeia

The following extract is from Katherine Mansfield's short story *At The Bay*. Read the passage carefully and appreciate her fine use of words. Then complete the task below.

> Ah-Aah! sounded the sleepy sea. And from the bush there came the sound of little streams flowing, quickly, lightly, slipping between the smooth stones, gushing into ferny basins and out again; and there was the splashing of big drops on large leaves, and something else – what was it? – a faint stirring and shaking, the snapping of a twig and then such silence that it seemed some one was listening.

ISBN 9780170195959

Round the corner of Crescent Bay, between the piled-up masses of broken rock, a flock of sheep came pattering. They were huddled together, a small, tossing, woolly mass, and their thin, stick-like legs trotted along quickly as if the cold and the quiet had frightened them. Behind them an old sheep-dog, his soaking paws covered with sand, ran along with his nose to the ground, but carelessly, as if thinking of something else. And then in the rocky gateway the shepherd himself appeared. He was a lean, upright old man, in a frieze coat that was covered with a web of tiny drops, velvet trousers tied under the knee, and a wide-awake with a folded blue handkerchief round the brim. One hand was crammed into his belt, the other grasped a beautifully smooth yellow stick.

1   Let's start with the individual figures of speech. Highlight and then list one example of each of these figures of speech. Alongside try to explain the effect of each one.

   a   simile   _____

   b   metaphor   _____

   c   alliteration   _____

   d   onomatopoeia   _____

   e   assonance   _____

   f   rhythm   _____

2   Now, using what you have observed in Katherine Mansfield's writing, explain the overall effect she is creating in this passage. You might like to think about early mornings in the bush or by the sea that you have experienced yourself.

   _____

   _____

   _____

   _____

An extended metaphor is where a metaphor is extended (developed) over a passage or throughout a poem.

This next poem extends a metaphor. The poet, Richard Wilbur, is writing about his daughter. Carefully read the poem and answer the questions that follow.

The Writer

In her room at the prow of the house
Where light breaks, and the windows are tossed with linden*,
My daughter is writing a story.

I pause in the stairwell, hearing
From her shut door a commotion of typewriter-keys
Like a chain hauled over a gunwale.

Young as she is, the stuff
Of her life is a great cargo, and some of it heavy:
I wish her a lucky passage.

ISBN 9780170195959

1   Can you explain what **metaphor** the poet has chosen and how verses 2 and 3 extend this metaphor?

_____

_____

_____

_____

_____

_____

_____

_____

_____

_____

_____

_____

_____

2   Explain, in as much detail as you can, the effect of this particular comparison.

_____

_____

_____

_____

_____

_____

_____

A euphemism expresses an unpleasant, or uncomfortable or, embarrassing situation in a more sensitive, kind and tactful manner.

Which phrase is a **euphemism**? Circle the correct answer.

1	Hayley eats like a sparrow.	Yes	No
2	The sick cat sat on the silky cushion.	Yes	No
3	His shoes have seen better days.	Yes	No
4	The wind swept up the autumn leaves into a tidy pile.	Yes	No

A pun is a clever play on words which are similar in sound but different in meaning.

Try to complete each of the following **puns**.

1   Skipping school to bungy jump will get you _____.

2   On the shelf there are three maths books, two English books and the rest is _____.

3   Our social studies teacher says her globe means the _____ to her.

4   It wasn't school Tony disliked, it was just the _____ of it.

5   When the electricity went off at school the students were _____-_____.

ISBN 9780170195959

Use the essay below to complete the activity on pages 102–103 of *How to … Achieve in Year 10 English*.

That Outdoor Education should be a compulsory subject for Years 9–13

In today's society the message is that our young people are too fat. Teenagers are bombarded with pressure to be thinner and fitter. Physical activity is an important part of the school curriculum, and if it were made compulsory we would see many benefits for all students right through to Year 13. Whether it is in the form of traditional Physical Education or the newer Outdoor Education, getting students outdoors and involved in physical activity can only encourage them to be healthy in other aspects of life, help develop their social skills and offer them a break from the academic load.

If Outdoor Education were compulsory for every student there would not be so many with weight issues. Taking a school subject that requires students to be involved in physical activity will help to burn calories. By spending time kayaking, running down to the beach for a swim or taking part in a game of touch rugby or dodge ball students are getting some exercise. The Push Play guidelines suggest 30 minutes each day. By taking part in an Outdoor Education class students are meeting these recommendations and this would also encourage students to continue being healthy and exercising outside of school hours.

Outdoor Education also helps to develop students' social skills. By playing sports and fun games, students learn to trust and work together with their teammates. You can't win team sports as an individual or abseil on your own, so students learn to work alongside others. These activities also teach students perseverance as they involve skills that are learnt by practice. Many times students will also have to face a challenge. It may be learning to rock climb or to throw with accuracy. This will be beneficial later in life as they enter the workforce, as they will have the confidence to tackle new tasks and stick with them. All of this means they build respect for themselves and for other people.

Regular exercise for teenagers is important but schools seem to focus more on the academic side of school. Outdoor Education is not only a time where students can get fit, but it is also a break from students' academic workload. Outdoor Education can be seen as a time when students get to relax and enjoy themselves. It is important to have this balance, which reduces stress and pressure. If outdoor education were compulsory for students in years 9–13, when the academic load is heaviest, students would be able to have some 'time-out' from schoolwork and regain their focus and energy.

By making Outdoor Education compulsory we are encouraging students to stay fit and healthy. We are teaching them skills that are beneficial to both their current lifestyle and their future careers. Young adults will also benefit greatly from their reduced stress levels. It is important for teenagers to have access to regular exercise so students should be required to include "Outdoor Ed" in their subject selection for their own well-being.

Use the speech below to complete the activity on pages 93-94 of *How to ... Achieve in Year 10 English.*

Repetition of phrase/sentence structure.

Personal prounoun, tells the audience that it is the writer's opinion.

Alliteration for flow.

Forget about crime dramas; forget about the CSI franchise, it seems to me that Reality TV is taking over our television screens. Bottle blondes, fake suntans, tension and tears. From home renovations to wannabe popstars, filthy houses to extreme makeovers, bug-covered, mould-growing pizzas and well, lots more home renovations, our TV screens are awash with 'reality'.

Before I go any further let's stop and work out exactly what Reality TV is. From my viewing experience I think that it is a genre in which the fortunes of 'real life' people (as opposed to fictional characters played by actors) are followed. Where people are put into difficult situations and are made to push their limits, usually to win money and sometimes more importantly the fame they will be awarded with afterwards.

Who is it that watches Reality TV? I hear you all internally saying 'not me'. But I imagine it would be difficult to find one person in this room who does not watch at least one reality TV programme a week. How do I know this? I asked around of course. Having talked to 45 people may not make me an expert but it does give us a fair indication of who is watching what. It seems that Reality TV is viewed by a cross spectrum of ages. However as expected the 10-15 year olds watched the most!

On the whole, the younger age group watched programmes that are considered 'trashy'. The ones that relied on looks, peer pressure and bimbos to survive ie. *The Simple Life* and *Outback Jack* – hardly brainteasers. On the other hand the older age brackets watched the 'thinking' programmes, for instance *The Amazing Race*, *The Apprentice* and *Dancing with the Stars*. The most interesting thing to come from out of this is the fact that *Fear Factor* was the only programme watched by ALL age groups. Except those with weak stomachs of course!

As much as they appear to be harmless, all-in-good-fun sort of programmes there is an ugly side of Reality TV that we can't escape. The fame the contestants all relished in the beginning seems to tarnish rather quickly. And of course depending how they edit the programme is how you are portrayed to the nation and beyond.

Colloquial language to make it 'chatty' and appealing.

Personal prounoun, tells the audience that it is the writer's opinion.

Rhetorical question to get the audience thinking about the speech and therefore involving them and making them want to continue listening.

Use of statistics to show she has some factual basis for her claims.

Yet another unfortunate side effect of Reality TV has been the fight to get bigger, better, more dramatic programmes and this is beginning to have some seriously negative implications. The American talk-show *Jenny Jones* had a programme topic 'People who had Secret Crushes on other People'. Relatively bizarre that you would want to go on national television to lay it all out but of course there had to be that twist to make it 'watchable' - they were same sex crushes and some of the guests weren't told about this. A male competitor found out that his male friend had a crush on him and exploded giving the programme the ratings they wanted. Later in the 'real world' the 'explosion' turned into murder leaving the competitor dead and the other serving a life sentence.

Several incidents have also happened in our own country that give programmes of this nature a bad name. A contestant, Mahesh Muralidhar, was competing in the now cancelled show *Going Straight*. His challenge involved walking through a minefield of pyrotechnic devices. The original stunt was successfully completed BUT they requested a second attempt for better camera angles. This time the only protection he was given was a crash helmet and the safety officer was not even present. Mr Muralidhar suffered second and third degree burns to at least 12% of his body after one of the devices exploded underneath him. What a prize! Not!

Of course you've all heard over and over again the Lana Coc-Kroft story. A quick recap: *Celebrity Treasure Island 2004*, coral cut, felt a bit sick, got a lot worse, evacuated from sunny Fiji in a critical condition, near death experience, months of rehabilitation. It is widely acknowledged that had she been provided with the correct foot wear (only $5 from The Warehouse) for the dangerous coral she would never have been exposed to the toxic syndrome in the first place.

The list of unsuccessful and/or weird Reality TV programmes goes on. I'm sure you could all share a story you've read somewhere or heard somewhere about that reality TV genre. Judges harsh comments being responsible for a suicide, Drew Barrymore talking someone out of having plastic surgery to look just like her, the list goes on. I think it is fair to say that sometimes Reality TV shows go too far.

Considering the complaints we hear everyday about the sheer volume of increasingly ridiculous Reality TV programmes it amazes me that people of all ages are more than happy to sit down and watch their fair share. If we are to force television producers into making better quality programmes perhaps we simply need to switch our television sets off. But then again, those bottle blondes, fake suntans, tension and tears are more than a little gripping. What are YOU going to watch tonight?

ISBN 9780170195959

Use the grid below to help you plan the story you are asked to write on pages 136-137 of *How to ... Achieve in Year 10 English.*

A story in five paragraphs

TELL	ADD	SHOW (aim for 20 words)	Our Example	Your Example
Para 1 Setting	Time and place.	Time of day, weather, what place looks like, sounds that can be heard, atmosphere, mood.	Night, frosty, moon gleams on water, beach, empty, occasional scurrying sound of creature in the grasses.	
Para 2 Main character	The person you put at the centre of the story.	Gender, age, clothes, appearance, attitude.	Sam, old man, shirts and heavy colourful but washed out sweater, beanie, carrying sack, striding along head up, whistling.	
Para 3 An event	Something happens. Does not have to be momentous, could be everyday event or unusual one.	What could happen? Another person appears? Something is lost/found? Character's feelings/thoughts? Something goes well/ badly?	Sudden barking noise from behind. Sam turns and whistles back. Out of darkness dog appears. Collie. Old too. Approaches man limping. Sam sighs, is annoyed.	
Para 4 The climax	Most exciting or dramatic part.	Accident? Argument? Something frightening? Surprising?	Child appears. About 8. Female, dressed in nightclothes and bare feet. Calls 'Don't go!' Man pulls dog towards child.	
Para 5 The ending	The ending.	Tie up loose ends. Problem solved? Character learns something?	Hands collar to child and encourages her to hold on. Kisses both of them and turns to walk away. Then changes mind and goes back holding child's hand.	

ISBN 9780170195959

Use the diagram below to help you plan your research from pages 168-169 of *How to ... Achieve in Year 10 English.*

The Research Process

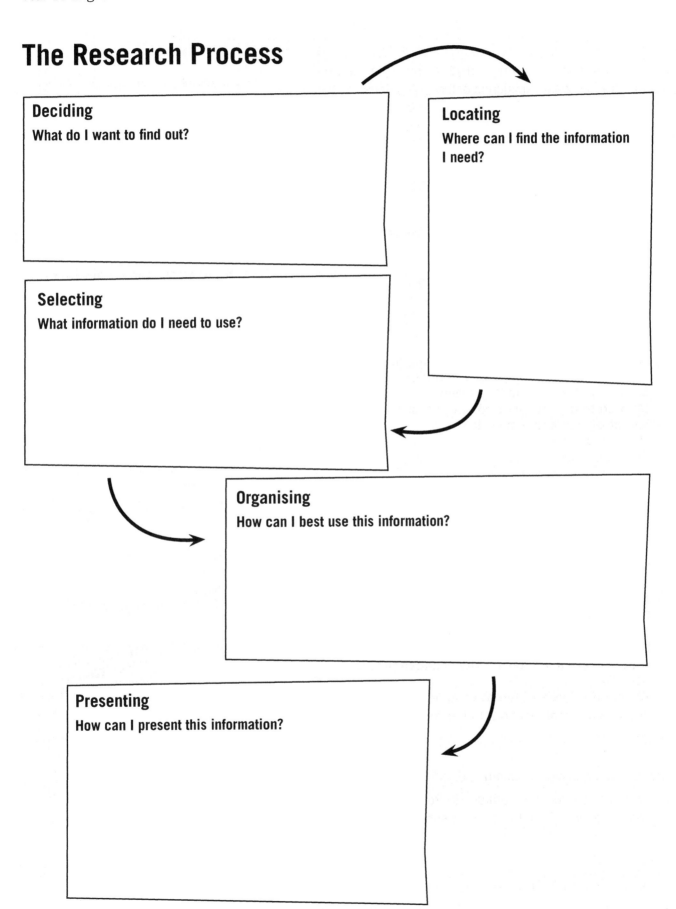

Deciding

What do I want to find out?

Locating

Where can I find the information I need?

Selecting

What information do I need to use?

Organising

How can I best use this information?

Presenting

How can I present this information?

Week _____ Date for completion _____

Parent's sig. _____ Teacher's sig. _____

Lyrics are like poetry. They have rhythm and rhyme and often draw on the personal experience of the writer/singer. In these lyrics, the singer Robbie Williams is remembering a particular teacher at his school and imagining meeting him again. This is what he wants to tell that teacher.

Hello sir, remember me?
I'm the man you thought I'd never be.
The boy who you reduced to tears,
The lad called Thingy for six whole years.
Yeah, that's right,
My name's Bob,
The one who landed the popstar's job.
The one who you told "look don't touch"
The kid who wouldn't amount to much.
Well, I'm here,
And you're still there,
With your fake sportscar and receding hair,
Dodgy pair of trousers, that you think are smart.
Married to the woman that teaches art.
Married to the life, married to the school.
I want to sing and dance sir.
Now, who's the fool?
Sing and dance,
You thought I was barmy.
"Settle down Thingy, join the army."
And who are you to tell me this?
The dream I want I'll have to miss.
Sir is God, he's given the right,
To structure lives overnight.
Now I know life's true path,
Tanks and guns, that'll be a laugh.
No, not me.
I'm a megacivilian.
I won't lead my life riding pillion.
But thanks for the advice
And I'm sure it will do, for the negative people
Just like you.
As for now, I've a different weapon,
Stage and screen is about to beckon.

Robbie Williams

Do you remember the process for analysing a poem?

Step 1: Read – preferably aloud.
Step 2: Reread quietly, take in main ideas.
Step 3: Use a dictionary to help you with difficult vocabulary.
Step 4: Read again.
Step 5: Highlight poetic techniques.
Step 6: Discuss as a class/in pairs.
Step 7: Now you have all the information, reread the poem. Enjoy it!
Step 8: Answer any questions that follow.

You will need to look up the highlighted words in order to fully understand this poem.

- receding
- dodgy
- fool
- barmy
- pillion

Locate the following techniques by underlining and annotating beside the poem.

- Rhetorical question
- Personal pronoun
- Rhyme
- Irony
- Cliché
- Metaphor
- Repetition
- Emphasis

You can listen to Robbie Williams read this poem approximately 10 minutes after the end of track 13 of his 'Ego has Landed' CD.

Answer each question in as much detail as possible.

1 What was the teacher's attitude to Robbie Williams when Robbie was at school? Quote two lines from the poem to support your answer.

_____

_____

2 What career did Robbie Williams dream of having?

_____

ISBN 9780170195959

3 What career did the teacher suggest he should take up?

_____

4 What do you think is meant by the line 'I won't live my life riding pillion'?

_____

_____

5 Robbie Williams has made up the word 'megacivilian'. What do you think it means?

_____

_____

6 How does Williams suggest the teacher's life is unsuccessful?

_____

_____

7 In your own words explain why you think Robbie Williams wrote this poem. What is he trying to say to the teacher he had?

_____

_____

8 Find two examples of colloquial language from the poem.

_____

9 Find two examples of rhyme from the poem.

_____

10 Give the poem a suitable title.

_____

Use a capital letter for:
- the start of every new sentence
- using the word 'I'
- days of the week
- months of the year
- names of people, places
- important words in the title of books, television programmes and films.

Use a full stop at:
- the end of every sentence.

Use an apostrophe to:
- show ownership
- show where letters are missed out in a contraction.

Use a comma to:
- divide a sentence into parts, making the ideas easier to identify
- separate items in a list.

Use speech marks to:
- identify words that are actually spoken
- new speaker: new line.
Remember that all the punctuation belonging to the spoken words goes inside the speech marks!

Correct the following paragraph, putting in the correct punctuation. It might be a good idea to start in pencil. Mark where a new line would begin with a slash (/).

six minutes later sandwiches in hand they were on the beach just east of their home the sea was calm its waves lapped gently along the shoreline and a few scruffy seagulls hopped about in the shallows I dont want to paddle wailed susie its cold dont be a wimp said tom youve got your gumboots on theyre not mine theyre janes susie pouted jane wished herself back on her bed reading her book

ISBN 9780170195959

Focus 1: Creating character notes

You will be asked to discuss/write about the main characters in any text you study.
It will be a lot easier to do this if you have first prepared some notes. Try using the following questions to form notes for the main character in the text you are currently studying in class.

Personality: Cheerful? Sad? Lonely? Think about any changes that occur and why.
_____
_____
_____
_____

Appearance: What do they look like? Think about the clues given to their character by: clothing/hair/distinguishing features and so on.
_____
_____
_____
_____

Behaviour: How do they act and react to events? We always judge people by their actions, what do the characters actions say about them?
_____
_____
_____
_____

Speech: How do they talk? What clues does it give us about who they are? Their age? The setting? Does this change between relationships?
_____
_____
_____
_____

Motivation: Why is the character doing what they are doing? Why are they reacting as they are? What is pushing them down the path they take? Fear? The desire to do what is right? Peer pressure?
_____
_____
_____
_____

Interaction with others: List the significant relationships your character has throughout the book. Think about if they contrast, show conflict etc. For each write down the importance of the relationship to the main character and the events that occur in the text.
_____
_____
_____
_____

Relevance to theme/s: How does the character help us to understand what the author/director is trying to say? Think about their actions, changes in attitudes, realisations etc.
_____
_____
_____
_____

Changes that occur to them: Do they change their appearance/actions/attitudes? If so why? What happened to bring about the change? An event? An action taken by someone else? A realisation?
_____
_____
_____

Role-modelling qualities: What can we learn from them/their actions/attitudes?
_____
_____
_____
_____

We thought that we would remind you about the ins and outs of writing a formal paragraph early on in the text. This structure can be used in essays across all your subjects: Science, Geography, Physical Education. We aren't teaching you rocket science – just a basic structure to ensure you can clearly and logically get your point across – whatever that point may be.

You should remember that paragraphs consist of several sentences which are arranged in a logical way to develop and explain a main idea.

- The **main idea** is stated in a single sentence – the **topic sentence**. Generally, the topic sentence is the first sentence of the paragraph.
- Other sentences explain and illustrate the main idea – they are the **explanatory sentences**. A sentence which does not contribute to the main idea should not be included – it is an **irrelevant sentence**.
- Explanations and **examples** in paragraphs are logically organised and linked by the use of **conjunctions**.
- A paragraph finishes with either a **concluding sentence**, which summarises the main idea; or a **linking sentence**, which leads to the next paragraph in an essay.

You do:

1 Identify the parts of a paragraph in the following paragraph by:
- underlining the topic sentence
- drawing a wavy line under the explanatory sentence/s
- highlighting the example sentence/s
- drawing a dotted line under the concluding sentence
- crossing out any irrelevant sentences.

> One of the main reasons students choose to study overseas is to learn about a culture first hand. Many students who have been studying a language at school choose to take a year between school and university to find out more about the country where that language came from. Others may choose to go to a country where the lifestyle is very different from their own so they can understand other people's lives. Making friends is also something that happens. A student who studied Spanish at school who travels to Spain will see how the language fits into the culture of the country. Everyone benefits from this sort of exchange of culture as the Kiwi learns to learn to live in the Spanish way and their Spanish hosts learn about Kiwi life.

2 This paragraph is in the wrong order. Put it in a better order by placing the corresponding number/s into the box below.

Topic Sentence	Explanation Sentence/s	Example Sentence/s	Conclusion Sentence

    Life in prison should be less attractive than life outside prison.

    If people break the law they should have to face harsher penalties in order to stop re-offending.

3   They no longer had access to television, computers etc while in their cells.

4   It seems unfair that prisoners should have access to some of the luxuries of life while in a prison for committing serious crimes, after all prison is just that – not a holiday.

5   In 2005 prison inmates chose to riot because privileges had been taken off them.

6   Why should these law breakers have the same access to televisions, computers and cellphones as law-abiding citizens?

ISBN 9780170195959

Foods are Written close reading

Making a meal of it

Every day more of us are too busy, too tired or too slack to prepare a meal, spawning an industry of people who do your cooking for you.

Hang around any city supermarket of an evening and you will see them. Mostly they are in well-cut suits, sporting sharp haircuts and extensive shoes that cannot quite compensate for a slightly harassed demeanour. Occasionally they are in tracksuit pants, baby on hip, and handbag spilling over the floor.

They are not here to figure out what to cook for dinner, but to see what has already been cooked for them. They are, of course, 21ˢᵗ-century people with an increasing interest in healthy, trendy food, but decreasing ability or inclination to prepare it themselves.

At a time when our televisions are crammed with celebrity cooking programmes, bookshops are groaning under the weight of the new recipe collections, and magazines devoted almost entirely to the topic are among our bestsellers, fewer of us actually cook every day.

Consumer research from ACNielsen shows only a quarter of us cook an evening meal seven nights a week and most of these are aged over 55. Half those surveyed who do cook a meal some nights reported using pre-prepared ingredients, a trend most noticeable among younger cooks.

Not only did ACNielsen report 'significant increases in sales of pre-prepared meals', but also a corresponding decrease in the sales of core ingredients such as butter, flour and sugar.

After all, how many of us know the correct way to dice an onion, or make a white sauce or gravy?

What we might call cooking – heating the pasta sauce and boiling the tortellini – is merely food assembly.

Such is the increasing demand for food that's already done for us, that cans of tomatoes are now pre-flavoured. Lots of Italian-, or Mexican-style, for example, frozen vegetables are already combined into stir-fry mixes and where once we thought opening a can of condensed soup was convenience, now we want the soup made and ready to heat. Ready-made soups, says Heinz Wattie marketing manager Mike Pretty, are now their biggest category, followed by pre-prepared sauces.

Of course there's a big difference between a can of condensed tomato soup and a soft-packed tomato and basil, or carrot and coriander variety. The latter frankly tastes a whole lot better than what a moderately gifted cook rustles up at home.

And that's probably the biggest change in convenience food – once the insipid pie, tired peas and grey watery potato removed from the box and eaten off a tray in front of Coronation Street symbolized a sad, pathetic lonely life.

Now, throwing the curry into the microwave, zapping the naan bread, cracking the foil on the pottle of hummus and tipping the salad into a bowl, is just so cool. No one even pretends they made any of this themselves.

That there is an increasing demand for trendy convenience food is, of course, because we are increasingly time-poor. We work longer hours than did our parents and women, especially, are no longer expected to derive their self-esteem from the stove-top. Add to that the fact supermarkets are open nearly all hours, and we have less need to plan our eating in advance.

You do:

Answer each question in as much detail as possible.

1 Within the headline and sub-heading there are four language techniques. Identify and give an example of each.

_____
_____
_____

2 The first sentence of the article talks about 'them'. In your own words explain who these people are.

_____

3 Why is there an increasing demand for convenience foods?

_____

ISBN 9780170195959

4 Even if we do cook, what has changed?

_____

_____

_____

5 What is the 'new' term for cooking?

_____

6 The image behind convenience foods has changed. Explain.

_____

_____

_____

7 Why is the central image blurred?

_____

_____

Whether you realise it or not, you are probably already an expert at using many different types or styles of language, in other words many 'registers'. The term 'register' simply describes the various styles of language available for writing or speaking – from the informal register of slang and swearing, to the formal academic register used when writing at university or professionally.

No register is right or wrong in itself. Correctness depends on the context of communication. Using slang is probably fine when relaxing with friends, but include it in a job application letter and don't hold your breath waiting for an interview.

The features which interconnect to determine the register of communication, oral or written, are: appropriateness, participants and their status, situation.

If you need more guidance on recognising different registers, refer to chapter 2 of your Year 10 How to … textbook.

Imagine you were late to school (how hard can that be!) because you had to rescue a dog that had been hit by a car. First you need to explain your lateness to the Dean. Then later at interval you are going to explain why you were late to your best mate.

The language you will choose will be different for each situation. One is more formal – with a person in authority, while the other is less formal – with one of your peers.

Conversation with your Dean	Conversation with your peer/friend

ISBN 9780170195959

UNIT 4

Week _____ Date for completion _____

Parent's sig. _____ Teacher's sig. _____

The purpose of this task is to persuade a parent/guardian to allow you to do something they do not want you to do. You will need to write a two minute speech that you will present to your parents, in which you attempt to win their permission.

Remember that your audience will be your parents – an audience opposed to what you have to say. You must speak directly to them and use forceful but respectful and appropriate language, to convince them of your side of the issue.

The topic we have chosen is:

I want to redecorate my room.

Ask your parents for a list of opposing arguments. The more arguments they provide, the easier your task will probably be. Show them your task – they'll be happy to help!

You must *address each opposing argument that they have given you*. Try to give reasons that refute what they have said. Be forceful, yet respectful . . . these are your parents!

When you have completed your speech, present it to your parents before handing it in along with the list of parental objections that formed the basis of your speech.

If your parents are really easy going and can't think of any objections, we offer some here –

Parental objections:

1   It's too expensive.

2   You never even clean your room; why decorate?

3   You already spend too much time there. We only see you at meals as it is now.

4   You never spend any time in your room; why should we bother?

5   Your brother (sister) is going to feel left out. We can't start redecorating everyone's room.

6   Your taste in interior decoration is questionable. We can't paint ceilings and walls in weird colours or graffiti.

7   I'll end up doing all the work. I don't have the time or the energy.

8   I said 'No!'

There will be others. ☺ Write the final copy of your speech in the back of this book.

> If you need more guidance on recognising different registers, refer to chapter 14 of your Year 10 *How to …* textbook.

Parental objections	My rebuttal

ISBN 9780170195959

Figures of speech are used to create images (pictures) in the mind of the reader. This poem by James Kirkup does so very successfully. It is illustrating the effect of an electrical storm on the place and people who experience it. It aims to create a rhythm that mirrors a fast-beating heart. Read it. Learn it off by heart. Annotate it as suggested to see how the poet has chosen great words to illustrate his theme.

Writing poetry that is regular in its metre and that rhymes is very difficult. Try it! Perhaps a four verse poem like this one about good weather…

Thunder and Lightning

Blood punches every vein
As lightning strips the windowpane

Under its flashing whip, a white
Village leaps to light.

On tubs of thunder, fists of rain
Slog it out of sight again.

Blood punches the heart with fright
As rain belts the village night.

1 Annotate the following around the poem:
- the hard consonants at the start of words
- the single syllable words
- alliteration
- violent verbs
- violent nouns
- personification
- metaphor.

2 Here are four frames, one for each verse of the poem. Draw what you can see.
   Our artist has completed the second one for you to give you an idea of what is possible.

Week _____ Date for completion _____

Parent's sig. _____ Teacher's sig. _____

HINT FOR SUCCESS
Use what you have learnt about structuring a formal or literary essay in other subjects that require you to write paragraph or essay answers.

This activity asks you to write a clear, detailed, thoughtful essay. Complete the information in the box below before you begin.

Title of text: Author of text:

Let's recap how to write a literary essay. Let's take a look at the topic you have been given:

Introduction	Body paragraphs	Conclusion
This paragraph should always: • give the title and author (director, poet) of the text • give the genre (novel, short story, poem, film) • refer to the question.	The body of the essay is divided into paragraphs. How many will depend on the type of question you are asked. Generally a body paragraph should have: • a topic sentence that clearly states what the paragraph will be about • detail from the text • relevant quotations • explanation • a sentence to link back to the original idea.	Will include: • no new information (it shows lack of prior planning) • a restatement of the main point of your essay, referring back to the question.

Let's have a look at the essay topic you have been given.

Describe the main challenge to a major character in your text and explain, giving detailed reasons, how the character responded to this challenge.

1   Using a red or blue pen annotate the question.
    • Put brackets around each part of the question.
    • Underline the key words in the question.

If you need more guidance on recognising different registers, refer to chapter 10 of your Year 10 *How to …* textbook.

2   On a scrap piece of paper decide upon the following things.
    • List the possible character/s and their challenge/s that you could use for this topic.
    • For each option you have come up with write brief notes on how the character responded. Was it well/sensible/irrational? Was it to be admired/avoided? Did you learn something from it?

3   Evaluate the information you have written down. One character and accompanying challenge should stand out as being easier to write about than the others.
    • Look through your handouts, character notes, and so on.
    • Go back to the key place in the text and re-read it. Take notes and copy suitable quotations.
    • Use a different-coloured pen to group and structure your information.

You should now be ready to begin writing your essay. Write the final copy of your essay in the back of this book.

You may have heard the term 'emotive language' while studying English. Do you know what the word emotive means? Just to be sure, use a good dictionary to find the definition of the following two words and write the definition in the space provided:

Emotion: _____

Emotive: _____

ISBN 9780170195959

By now you will have worked out that emotive language has something to do with 'arousing emotion'. Authors work hard to create an atmosphere, mood or tone in their writing. To do this they carefully choose the **vocabulary** they use. To influence people writers choose emotive words instead of neutral words. For example:

The child climbed over the fence. *(neutral)*

Could become:

The ragamuffin scrambled over the barbed wire fence. *(emotive)*

The sentence becomes more emotive because we have used detail and chosen words that have different connotations.

You do:

1   Decide which sentence is neutral and which is emotive.

Jenna is thin. _____   Jenna is skinny. _____

2   Rewrite the following sentences to make them more emotive by changing no more than two words in each one.

a   The girl ate her sandwich.

_____

b   A big boy walked across the paddock.

_____

c   The hungry dog scratched at the door to the kitchen.

_____

d   A wind blew the curtains about.

_____

e   Anna went out quietly.

_____

f   Adam closed the door firmly.

_____

3   It can be fun to overdo things. Romance writers and writers of thrillers often get accused of 'laying it on with a trowel'. Finish one of the following paragraphs in what would be criticised as an overblown style if we weren't asking you to do it on purpose. (Every year there's a worldwide competition for the worst beginning to a novel... maybe you'll win it!)

1   Raven leaned languidly on the balcony's marble rim, her silky black hair glistening in the soft moonlight as her ocean-deep blue eyes gazed longingly....

Or 2   Jake, his expensive overcoat slung over his broad shoulders and his fedora perched nonchalantly on his blond curls, whistled quietly as he crossed the dark deserted street on the bad side of town.

Or 3   Make up one of your own based on the kind of writing you find overwritten e.g. science fiction or westerns or soaps or ...

_____

_____

_____

_____

_____

_____

_____

ISBN 9780170195959

Week _____ Date for completion _____

Parent's sig. _____ Teacher's sig. _____

Focus 1: Visual close reading

Read the advertisement through carefully and highlight/annotate the layout elements of a visual text.

Then look for as many examples of verbal techniques and visual techniques as you can possibly find. Make sure you do this tidily. Do not ruin your ability to see the overall image.

Layout	Visual techniques	Verbal techniques
• Headline	• Use of font	• Emotive language
• Image	• Logo	• Imperative
• Body copy	• Use of empty space	• Personal pronoun
• Background	• Contrast	• Alliteration
• Logo/slogan	• Pencil drawing … made to look like jottings beside list	• Emphasis
• Balance		• Punctuation

In Unit 5 we looked at emotive language. You worked out that it is where writers work hard to create an atmosphere, mood or tone in their writing. To do this they carefully choose the vocabulary they use.

Look at the words/ phrases used in this advertisement:

Cut free/
tiny cage/wounds/
metal catheter
embedded/torture/
doesn't even
need …

All the words help to build a negative image of the life of captive Moon Bears. Try and become more aware of how vocabulary has been selected in things you are reading. It can only be beneficial to your own work.

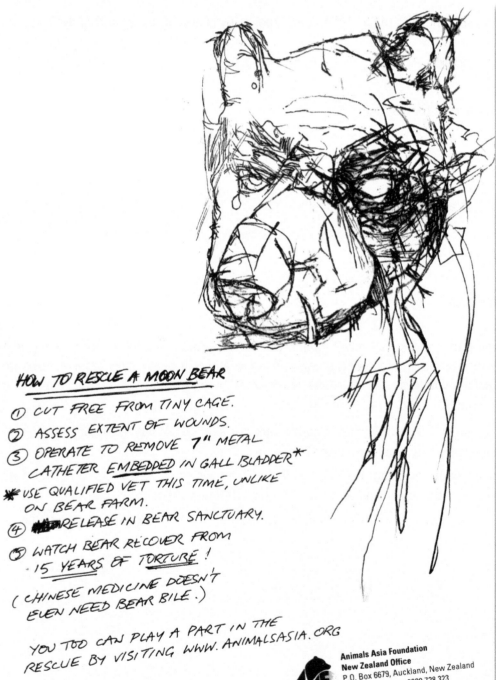

Answer each question in as much detail as possible.

1   This advertisement creates impact in a magazine as it has been hand drawn. Explain why.

_____

_____

Despite it being a somewhat simple advertisement it is no less effective. Let's look more closely to understand why.

2   Why have they left the logo in typesetting (rather than hand drawn)?

_____

_____

3   Why is the logo on an angle?

_____

_____

4   Why have they chosen to write in note form?

_____

_____

5   How have they chosen to 'highlight' certain aspects of the body copy? For each technique you find explain why it has been employed at that particular place in the body copy.

_____

_____

6   Why have they included the bracket comment despite it technically not being about 'rescuing' the bears?

_____

_____

7   Look carefully at the sketch of the bear. How has it been made to look tortured?

_____

_____

8   What does AAF want you to do having seen this advertisement? Quote from the advert in your answer.

_____

_____

Here's a little problem that lots of students have with their writing – essentially they don't know when to STOP! Here's one way of looking at this problem:
You know that two simple complete sentences can be joined with a conjunction.

It was a sunny day, so I put on lots of sun block.

If you omit the conjunction and put nothing else in its place (like a semicolon) then the sentence is a run-on sentence. Essentially that is two sentences (or more) that have fused together. Like this:

It was a sunny day I put on sun block.

Using one of the following connecting words/techniques in each of the sentences below, make the sentences correct: **when, and, before, because, ;**.

1   The band was a rock band Elijah was the lead guitarist.
2   Marcus loves to ride his motorbike it is a bright red one.
3   We went to the movies James sat next to Mere.
4   My mum went to Wellington she had to see a doctor there.
5   Six buses went by the seventh one stopped to pick us up.

UNIT
7

Week _____ Date for completion _____
Parent's sig. _____ Teacher's sig. _____

HINT FOR SUCCESS
Remember a spell check function on a computer isn't infallible! It's always a good idea to read through your work to check that it is error free.

Structuring your essay

A formal essay needs a formal structure. Your writing will be more authoritative and convincing if it is well-arranged. Here is a reminder of a simple structure that you will find easy to follow when you are writing a formal essay.

- state the topic
- state your point of view (which side of the topic you are arguing)
- give the three main ideas you will use
- be interesting and convincing – believe in yourself!

- have no fewer than three ideas in three separate paragraphs.

- a topic sentence that states the idea
- an explanation saying in more detail what you meant in your topic sentence
- evidence that supports your explanation with an effective example, anecdote, statistic, quotation …
- a concluding connection to the topic.

- restate the main points of the essay
- reinforce the writer's attitude without giving any new information
- end with a strong, thought-provoking statement or question.

HOW to…

If you need more guidance on writing a formal essay, refer to chapter 7 of your Year 10 *How to …* textbook.

Tricks of the trade:
- use a dictionary
- use a thesaurus
- use a spell checker (machine and person)
- use an editor
- and for those elusive ideas – the brainstorm!

These are the essentials:
- correct spelling
- correct paragraphing
- correct use of punctuation
- correct sentence structure.

And the ideals:
- expressive vocabulary
- good organisation or structure
- great ideas

Don't forget:
Try to imagine your essay is the last thing that the person making the final decision on your issue will read and it should therefore persuade them to agree with your opinion.

Your task is to write a formal essay on the topic:

> **That holidays/celebrations such as Easter, Valentine's Day, Christmas, Father's Day etc have become too commercialised.**

A brainstorm of points has been compiled to help you with your initial thinking and planning. Of course you may like to add to this information by talking to your parents and/or grandparents, by using the Internet or books in the library etc.

Feel free to argue whichever side of the issue you like.

We have given you a list of points to do with this topic. Use two different coloured highlighters to separate them into pros and cons.

We have also left some blank ovals for you to add your own ideas.

Multicultural society – why single out some customs and not others.

Retail workers are not free to enjoy the event (despite the fact their bosses must be raking it in!).

Places such as The Warehouse have made millions off commercialising these events.

Lots of people want to shop on holiday weekends – Easter is a great time for gardeners to shop for example.

Students want to work on holiday days to earn for the term time expenses.

Religious events are largely ignored. Christ's birthday/death are overshadowed by Santa and Easter Eggs. Even if not practising Christians it is time to stop and reflect on the meaning of life and our morals and values.

All about choice - people don't HAVE to go shopping.

Places more financial strain on people.

People don't HAVE to buy expensive gifts, they can agree to homemade gifts only or $10 limits.

It's lovely to see decorations up in the streets and stores.

ISBN 9780170195959

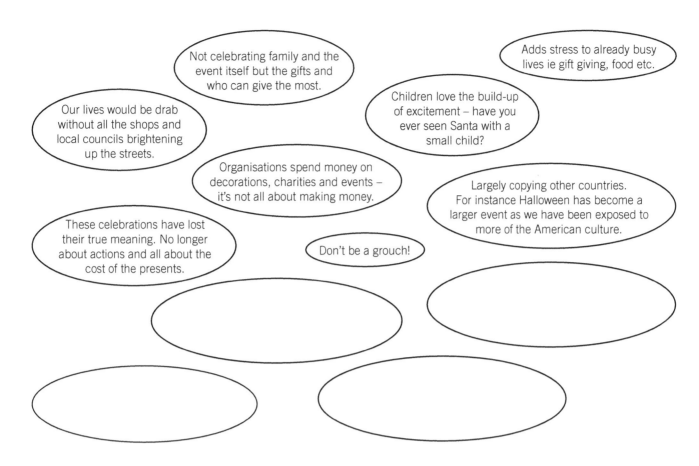

Write the final copy of your essay in the back of this book.

We like this attempt at explaining how the two punctuation marks are different when they separate clauses.

: The colon is like a springboard: you land on it and are propelled forwards.

; The semicolon is like the pivot of a seesaw: it enables two sides to balance each other.

Decide whether the phrases are equally balanced (semicolon) or have one phrase leading on to another (colon).

Each sentence needs a colon or a semicolon (or both). Put them in.

1   I wrote a letter to Santa and asked for __ a new bike, with red handlebars __ a torch, with rechargeable batteries __ a book about dinosaurs and a big box of chocolate fish.

2   The policeman spoke very slowly __ 'Do you understand me?' he asked.

3   The gate opened onto a green paddock __ it was full of sheep.

4   The gate opened onto a green paddock __ we walked through and the sheep scattered.

5   We raced to the cliff edge, gazed over the edge and gasped in horror __ there was the bike at the bottom.

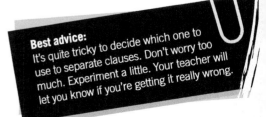

Best advice:
It's quite tricky to decide which one to use to separate clauses. Don't worry too much. Experiment a little. Your teacher will let you know if you're getting it really wrong.

Week _____ Date for completion _____

Parent's sig. _____ Teacher's sig. _____

Focus 1: Oral close reading

> Make no mistake, Madam Chair, my team and I are committed to the idea of law and order, no matter what has been said. We know, as you do my fellow citizens, that sometimes people need to be forced to do the right thing or persuaded to do the right thing. The cop car on the side of the road persuades us to slow down. The threat of a taser makes the knife-wielding P-taking thief drop his weapon. But this is not the same thing as a nuclear deterrent.
>
> Building nuclear weapons is not the right thing. Building nuclear weapons is most definitely the wrong thing. Your world is a fragile, delicately balanced mechanism. My world is a place where plants grow, animals live, and humans thrive. Our world is worth preserving. Building nuclear weapons, which simply destroy everything, is not the right thing… is not the sane thing to do.

Answer each question in as much detail as possible.

1 How can you tell this is part of a debate?_____

_____

2 How can you tell it is not the beginning of the debate?_____

_____

3 The speaker has included colloquial language. Identify the word and explain why it has been used.

_____

_____

4 What examples does the speaker use to support his claim to be in favour of law and order?

_____

_____

5 How does he build his case in paragraph 2?_____

_____

6 Why are ellipsis marks used?_____

_____

7 Identify three emotive words. Explain why they are powerful._____

_____

_____

_____

8 Choose four words in the passage that would be stressed. Explain your reasoning.

_____

_____

_____

_____

Put simply: Literal language means exactly what it says.

                 Figurative language doesn't mean exactly what it says.

For example: *My new computer has all the bells and whistles possible!*

The person is not saying that there are *literally* bells and whistles on the computer. Rather they are saying that the computer has flat screen, lots of memory, a dvd burner, an amazing video card, a wireless keyboard and mouse, Bluetooth etc.

Figurative language contains images. The writer or speaker describes something through the use of comparisons, for effect, interest, and to make things clearer. The result of using this technique is the creation of interesting images, which appeal to our imagination, asking us to look at our world in different ways. Clever comparisons, showing unusual similarities, add interest and perhaps even surprise us.

Here's a sentence from the novel *The God of Small Things* by Arundhati Roy. She is writing about heavy rain:

> 'Slanting silver ropes slammed into loose earth, ploughing it up like gunfire.'

This, we are sure, conjures up a picture in your mind of how the rain looks as it falls and its effect on the earth where it falls.

However, English is FULL of figurative language and some of these images are like a type of shorthand – we hear them so often we don't notice them. There are probably no surprises in this list:

simile:	Man, my new car is as quick as lightning.
metaphor:	You're such an airhead, Megan!
cliché:	In order to get my assignment done, I'll have to burn the midnight oil.
personification:	The gods must have been smiling on me today!
hyperbole (exaggeration):	I am sooo hungry I could eat a horse!

You do:

Turn each of these well-known figurative phrases into literal ones:

1   I got an Excellence for my essay – **I am over the moon**._____

2   His life is not **a bed of roses**._____

3   He **poisoned her mind** against me._____

4   Their argument is just **a storm in a teacup**._____

5   I'll do the dishes – **sweet as**._____

Now try it the other way. Here are five literal sentences. Rephrase them in figurative language. If you can make up your own, that's wonderful; but if not go for some you've already heard.

1   The ship sailed across the stormy ocean.

_____

2   Riding a horse is something you never forget how to do.

_____

3   I ate so much food at lunch that I am not at all hungry now.

_____

4   A slight breeze made the sail move just a little.

_____

5   Rain fell gently.

_____

Week _____ Date for completion _____

Parent's sig. _____ Teacher's sig. _____

The Old Place

No one comes
by way of the doughy track
through straggly tea tree bush
and gorse, past the hidden spring
and bitter cress.

Under the chill moon's light
no one cares to look upon
the drunken fence-posts
and the gate white with moss.

No one except the wind
saw the old place
make her final curtsy
to the sky and earth:

and in no protesting sense
did iron and barbed wire
ease to the rust's invasion
nor twang more tautly
to the wind's slap and scream.

On the cream-lorry
or morning paper van
no one comes,
for no one will ever leave
the golden city on the fussy train;
and there will be no more waiting
on the hill beside the quiet tree
where the old place falters
because no one comes any more

no one.

Hone Tuwhare

Do you remember the process for analysing a poem?
Step 1: Read – preferably aloud.
Step 2: Reread quietly, take in main ideas.
Step 3: Use a dictionary to help you with difficult vocabulary.
Step 4: Read again.
Step 5: Highlight poetic techniques.
Step 6: Discuss as a class/in pairs.
Step 7: Now you have all the information, reread the poem. Enjoy it!
Step 8: Answer any questions that follow.

You will need to look up the highlighted words in order to fully understand this poem.
- doughy
- straggly
- curtsy
- tautly
- falters

Locate the following techniques by underlining and annotating beside the poem.
- Repetition
- Personification
- Metaphor
- Onomatopoeia
- Alliteration

Answer each question in as much detail as possible.

1 How do you know this is a New Zealand poem?_____

_____

2 Look carefully at the first two verses of the poem. Which words does the poet choose to create atmosphere?

_____

3 Why is the fourth verse in italics?_____

_____

4 Why, does the poet suggest, that the house has been deserted?

_____

_____

5 Comment on the last two words of the poem.

_____

_____

_____

ISBN 9780170195959

You know that a **pronoun** is a word that stands in place of a noun. Pro- as a prefix means acting as a substitute for (rather than having turned professional if you like to keep a sporting metaphor in mind!).

But what does **reflexive** mean? Think about a reflex angle in maths, think about the idea of turned, reflected, bent backwards. A reflexive pronoun refers back to the subject. For example:

I gave **myself** a stern telling off.

Subject (who is doing the telling off): **I**

Object (who is receiving the telling off): **myself**

1   Fill in the grid with the correct matching reflexive pronoun. (Test your answer by putting the pronouns into the sentence above. You gave … a stern telling off.)

Subject pronoun	Reflexive pronoun	Subject pronoun	Reflexive pronoun
I	_____myself_____	It	_____
You	_____	We	_____
He	_____	You (plural)	_____
She	_____	They	_____

2   Try putting the correct reflexive pronoun into these sentences:
   a)   He whispered words of confidence to _____.
   b)   They gathered on the field by _____.
   c)   She remembered, she had drunk the lemonade _____.
   d)   We asked _____ the important question: why?
   e)   You will all go to the pool by _____.

Sometimes a reflexive pronoun is used for **emphasis** e.g. *He himself was to blame.*

3   Add a reflexive pronoun for emphasis to these sentences:
   a)   I _____ simply cannot learn French but I know others can.
   b)   You _____ are the best speaker in class.
   c)   She _____ was the only survivor of the singing competition.
   d)   They _____ were the winners of the debating competition.
   e)   You _____ are the finest group of marching girls in the country.

You know that pronoun means a word that substitutes for a noun, but what does **possessive** mean?

Think about possession, ownership. When you possess something you own it. So a possessive pronoun is one that shows ownership.

Here they are: **mine, yours, his, hers, its, ours, theirs.**

Whose is this umbrella?   It is _____ (*yours* or *mine? his* or *hers? ours* or *theirs?*)

4   Put the correct possessive pronoun in the spaces provided.
   a)   Which bag is ____ ? (your bag)
   b)   We've been to your house, would you like to come to _____ (our house)
   c)   I've finished my homework. Shall I help with ____ (your homework)
   d)   We drove to the party in our car; they went in _____ (their car)
   e)   He spoke using his notes; she didn't use _____ (her notes)

Please note there are no apostrophes in these possessive pronouns!

ISBN 9780170195959

Week _____ Date for completion _____

Parent's sig. _____ Teacher's sig. _____

When you write creatively, your aim is to express yourself in a simple, accurate and interesting manner. It's not always easy to get a great idea, to shape it effectively and write a brilliant story or poem or essay. But we know that practice helps!

Let's remind ourselves about the process of writing a successful piece of descriptive writing. Remember the way we used a small piece of chocolate to stimulate some great writing in your How To ... textbook (see page 133 if you want a reminder). We're going to ask you to try to do the same process by yourself this time – with that most essential of all liquids – water.

Water, water, everywhere and just a drop to drink. (to paraphrase S T Coleridge!)

Water … we clean our teeth with it, we wash ourselves in it, we use it to quench a real thirst and we drink it when Mum bans the sweeter drinks. But do we really appreciate its finer qualities?

Pour cold water into a clear glass and set it in front of you. Now, using all your senses, appreciate it, making notes as you go:

SIGHT   Have a careful look at the water, swill it round and see what effect this movement has.

_____

_____

_____

SMELL   Take a moment to think about the 'smell' of water. Put your nose in the top of the glass and breathe in deeply. How would you describe its aroma?

_____

_____

_____

TOUCH   Can you 'feel' the glass holding the water? Is it cool? Dip the tip of your finger into the water.

_____

_____

_____

TASTE   Take a sip of the water, let it roll around your mouth and think about its texture and taste.

_____

_____

_____

TASTE/ TOUCH   Take a long swallow and describe the feel of the water as it goes down your throat.

_____

_____

_____

Now, using the notes you have made, try writing a paragraph about drinking water. Choose your setting. A desert might be a bit of a cliché unless you've been to one recently, but a hot summer day on the beach might be a good idea, or after a surf in salt water, after sports, first thing in the morning, when you get in from school etc.

Write the final copy of your writing in the back of this book.

ISBN 9780170195959

No doubt you will remember the unit of work on symbols and logos in your textbook (pages 78–81).

 ◄——— You will remember symbols like this one.

A logo is a design picture, a graphic or a word used
to convey information, or symbol for an organisation. ——►

Make your own business card

Imagine that it is 10 years in the future. You are about 25 years old, you've finished your education and training and you have set up your own business. You might be a florist, a photographer, a plumber, a lawyer, a hypnotist, an actor, an electrician, a builder, an accountant, a nurse, an astronaut (someone has to be one!).

You are going to design your own business card. It will be two-sided and contain some important information: your name, the name of your business, your contact details, your web site, your street address, your logo.

Here's an example of one made by a student:

Now design your own, make it on card and paste into the book or copy the details into the space provided.

The key components of a logo are:	Questions to think about when designing a symbol or logo:
• Main image • Dominant colour(s) i.e. to suggest particular moods • Proportion • Layout • How words are used in the logo (if they are used at all) • Link to the organisation	• Can the intended audience read and understand the sign? • Has colour been used effectively? • Does the overall design or shape of the sign or symbol, grab the client's attention? • If verbal features have been used, has the impact been through the use of upper case letters, lower case letters or the use of both? • If pictures have been used are they easily identifiable to the client?

Week _____ Date for completion _____

Parent's sig. _____ Teacher's sig. _____

Most of you will have a wide reading requirement as part of your study of English this year. This section has been designed to help you out with this. The idea of a wide reading programme is that it encourages you to read a variety of books through the year. This exposes you to many different styles of writing, opinions and subjects that you might not ordinarily see without such a programme.

Most of you will be required to hand in some sort of review of the books you have been reading. Look at the information below to help you.

What to remember about reviewing

Structure	Content
A review needs to be just long enough to give essential details and arouse curiosity. • Try to mention the name of the author and the book title in the first paragraph – there's nothing more frustrating than reading a review of a great book but not knowing who wrote it and what the title is! • Use one paragraph for each point you want to make about the book. • Try to get the main theme of the book across in the beginning of your review. Your reader should know right away what he or she is getting into should they choose to read the book! • What genre does your book belong to? Mystery? Adventure? Historical?	*Describe the setting of the text.* • How does it compare or contrast to the world you know? Does the author make you feel like you're a part of the setting? Can you picture the book's setting if you close your eyes? *Describe the book's main characters.* • Does the writer make you believe in them as people? Why or why not? • Think about whether you like the characters and about how liking them or disliking them makes you feel about the book. *Give your reader a taste of the plot, but don't give the surprises away.* • Readers want to know enough about what happens in a book to know whether they'll find it interesting. But they never want to know the ending! Summarise the plot in a way that will answer some questions about the book, but leave other questions in the reader's mind. *Make sure your review explains how you feel about the book and why, not just what the book is about.* • A good review should express the reviewer's opinion and persuade the reader to share it, to read the book, or to avoid reading it.

First things first … pick a book! You may already have one that you are reading or you may need to visit your school or local library and choose something that interests you. Using the above guidelines write a review for a book that you have read.

- Don't forget to check the specific requirements of your school wide reading programme if you are going to use this piece of writing as an assessment piece.
- If you are doing it for fun then swap your review with some of your peers and read what they have written about their reading. You might find a book to read!

- If you can't come up with a title on your own check with your librarian what is popular for students your age. Librarians are a wealth of information and know what is being issued regularly or is in demand.
- Alternatively consider one of these New Zealand authors.

Tessa Duder	Tania Roxborogh	Sheryl Jordan	Margaret Mahy	David Hill
Witi Ihimaera	Katherine Mansfield	Ken Catran	Owen Marshall	Maurice Gee
Paula Boock	Patricia Grace	Fleur Beale		

We want to remind you about these three parts of speech. Students sometimes get the adjective and the adverb confused. Although their role is similar, in that they add details to (or modify) other words, each one is linked to a different sort of word. Let's check that you know the difference.

Adjectives	Adverbs
Adjectives tell us more about nouns and pronouns. Adjectives add meaning to a noun or a pronoun as they give us more information about a word. They are often called describing words. They add interest and colour to sentences by describing or giving more information. For example: The sun disappeared behind the mountains. The **vivid orange** sun disappeared behind the **dark, brooding** mountains.	**Adverbs, are words that tell us more about verbs.** Adverbs, as their name suggests, add meaning to verbs (mostly). They answer the question 'How, when or where?' Let's look at how they do this. I walk **slowly**. (The adverb tells you *how* the person walks.) Other adverbs of manner are quickly, hungrily, fast. They usually end in –ly. Pay me back **tomorrow**. (The adverb tells you *when* the person should pay.) Other adverbs of time are soon, today, yesterday, never, immediately, now and again. The sky **above** is blue. (The adverb tells *where* the sky is.) Other adverbs of place are **here, there, nowhere, up, down, outside, inside, underneath, home, far** and **near**.

Now let's check you can apply this information. A few good adjectives and even fewer good adverbs are found in effective writing. Writers can overdo it – so note how *few* adverbs this piece contains.

> She edges to the right. That gives her about 2 centimetres before her shoulder butts against the rough wall. Her hand lands on something soft and she snatches it away. The toilet paper thuds to the floor.
>
> 'Why can't they have an inside toilet like normal people?' she mutters as she stretches her hand towards the paper. But it's too hard to reach. She inches forward, keeping an eye on the dark shape, and finally touches her fingers to the roll.
>
> There's a scuttling noise, and a monstrous shiny cockroach darts across the floor.
>
> Alice lets out a yelp.
>
> The cockroach runs blindly into a waiting web, and the spider hurries in for the kill.
>
> Alice grabs the toilet paper. She's done in record time, and her hand is on the latch before the paper even hits the bottom of the pit. And that's where her hand stays. She jiggles the latch, then pushes on the door, but it's firmly locked.
>
> Outside, there's a giggle.
>
> Alice's heart sinks. She should have known. She'd seen her cousins hanging around but was too rushed to worry about it.
>
> Her eyes dart back to the spider. It's bigger than Alice first thought, intent on its prey like a busy chef.
>
> 'Open the door!' she shouts.
>
> 'What's wrong, Alice?' comes Michael's voice. 'Having a bit of trouble?'
>
> *from* The Snake Pit, *by Sonya Bates*

1 Highlight all the adjectives and adverbs in the extract. Choose two, and in the space below, explain why you think the writer has chosen to use them.

2 Now highlight five effective **verbs**. Beside each one, explain what picture that verb creates for you.

_____

_____

_____

_____

Do you remember the other types of adjectives? Comparative and superlative adjectives? Go back to the first chapter of this book to check.

UNIT 12

Week _____ Date for completion _____

Parent's sig. _____ Teacher's sig. _____

A Letter to the Editor is a piece of persuasive writing, usually stemming from a matter of public interest that the writer feels very strongly about. Look at the boxes below to remind you of the format of these.

Structure of the letter

Your letter should:

- be organised logically
- be kept short – generally no more than 250 words
- have a forceful opening statement
- clearly present points of an argument to strengthen the main idea
- have a strong concluding statement.

Style of writing

Your letter writing should:

- use short sentences
- use short paragraphs (usually no more than two sentences)
- use emotive words to convey your attitude
- have a consistent tone (e.g. serious, amused, angry etc.)
- use formal language
- use straightforward vocabulary – a 12 year old should be able to understand it.

Content

Your letter should:

- put its most important message in the first paragraph
- be as factual as possible
- relate to local events, community
- be positive. If you criticise, also propose or champion a solution
- be about a current issue
- ask for action – tell the readers what you want done
- don't leave main points till the end - it is common practice for letters to be edited by cutting the last paragraph/s off.

You do:

Every local community has issues that are of interest. It might be: the lack of community facilities for young people, the need for roading changes, development of the beachfront, lack of schools, safety issues, theatre/teamsports/cinema/outdoor/indoor facilities.

Choose an issue that is important to you and your community and write a letter to the editor. You might even like to submit it to your community newspaper.

Write the final copy of your piece in the back of this book.

If you need more guidance on writing a Letter to the Editor, refer to chapter 8 of your Year 10 *How to ...* textbook.

The pantoum (*pan-toom*) originated in France during the 19th Century, based on a poetry form from Malaya. The pantoum's name derives from the Malayan word '*pantun*'.

Lots of people think of pantoums as circular but actually they are a spiral. You begin with a line, repeat lines on a set form and they somehow bring new meaning to the repeated lines. Then in the end you find you are back to the line you began with, but with a difference.

A pantoum poem is a fun format to play with. It looks like it is hard to do, but in actuality it is not. It follows a rhythmic pattern and is very easy to follow.

Look at the example below:

Writing my own pantoum.	1
The lines are all hopping about.	2
Why the first line goes where the last lines goes,	3
I don't think I can figure that out.	4
The lines are all hopping about.	2
Doesn't this thing need to rhyme?	5
I don't think I can figure that out.	4
Now the second line is the fifth line.	6
Doesn't this thing need to rhyme?	5
My brain is beginning to cramp.	7
Now the second line is the fifth line.	6
Who the hell's idea was that?	8
My brain is beginning to cramp.	7
Will my keyboard be melting down too?	9
Who the hell's idea was that?	8
I've been writing this poem since noon.	10
Will my keyboard be melting down too?	9
Tell me now, if anyone one knows.	11
I've been writing this poem since noon.	10
Will this riddle see me to my doom?	12
Tell me now, if anyone one knows.	11
Why the first line goes where the last line goes.	3
Will this riddle see me to my doom?	12
Writing my own pantoum.	1

ISBN 9780170195959

Now look at how a New Zealand poet used the structure of a pantoum to create a poem on New Zealand's bush.

Once you have read it through mark the line numbers down the right-hand side of the poem so you can see the revolving pattern of the lines.

A Pantoum in the New Zealand Bush

Is this not beautiful, she said
this colonnade of greenery
Cicadas sing and Bell birds ring
Above about and in between

This colonnade of greenery
Where Fantails skit and skite
Above about and in between
And water softens every sight

Where Fantails skit and skite
Delighting in our company
And water softens every sight
Yes this is beautiful indeed

Delighting in our company
Our togetherness together
Yes this is beautiful indeed
It may be paradise, she said

Our togetherness together
Cicadas sing and Bell birds ring
It may be paradise, she said
this colonnade of greenery

Sean Joyce

Just to let you know – this was the poet's tenth draft!

You guessed it … it is time for you to write your own pantoum. Just have fun with it!

We have given you a map of where the lines go to make it easier for you to create your own pantoum.

If you are not sure what to write about – start simply. Just look around your room or out your window and try creating a pantoum about what you see.

1 _____

2 _____

3 _____

4 _____

2 _____

5 _____

4 _____

6 _____

5 _____

7 _____

6 _____

8 _____

7 _____

9 _____

8 _____

10 _____

8 _____

3 _____

10 _____

1 _____

Week _____ Date for completion _____

Parent's sig. _____ Teacher's sig. _____

This extract is the beginning of a short story. Read it carefully.

The school inherited Alan after he left the neighbouring Boys' High. His reasons for leaving were never made entirely clear. As far as could be discovered, he hadn't actually been expelled, but his parents had been persuaded that it might be in everybody's best interests if Alan transferred his particular talents elsewhere. Alan's parents were easily persuaded to most things; they found it a lot less trouble than having to make their own decisions. Provided they looked suitably confused and willing to help, there was usually some forceful spirit around to tell them in which direction to move.

When he arrived, Alan turned out to be a second-year 6th former. He also turned out to be the most startlingly handsome boy the school had ever seen. The first time he walked down the corridor, he left parallel lines of girls gasping behind him like stranded dolphins. Slim, tanned, black-haired and hazel-eyed, he had a technique with females that made the battle-hardened Senior Mistress demand a chaperone whenever she interviewed him. To protect *him*, not *her*, she indicated.

Alan was totally charming and totally irresponsible. His single aim in life was to have a good time, and anything that interfered with this was either tolerated with an understanding smile or sidestepped smoothly. Work to Alan was one of those amusing irritants that some dour spirits spend their lives worrying about. As far as he was concerned, they were quite welcome to go around with their shoulders to the wheels, provided he could ride along on the axle.

Alan was never an actual discipline problem in class. He naturally didn't intend to do any work himself, but he had no objection to others getting on with it. Unfortunately, his effect upon those others was disastrous. The girls all wanted to mother him; the boys all wanted to smother him. By the time he'd been in any class for a week, the atmosphere was fairly crackling.

People in authority decided that Alan needed talking to.

Friendly Persuasion, David Hill

Look up the meanings of any words you don't understand. Do you know the meaning of *dour*? Of *chaperone*?

1 Annotate the passage where it shows:
  a the name of the main character
  b the physical appearance of the main character
  c words that have been emphasised
  d an example of alliteration
  e examples of metaphor (3!)
  f an example of repetition
  g an example of rhyme
  h words about the main character's personality
  i words about the main character's parents.

Now you have looked closely at the extract you will be able to write a very successful paragraph answer to this question:

2 Why is Alan a problem at school? Explain in as much detail as you can.

_____

_____

_____

_____

_____

This question is about tone.

3 Whose voice are you hearing? What kind of tone of voice do you think they are using as they tell Alan's story? Give reasons for your answer.

_____

_____

_____

ISBN 9780170195959

Have you noticed how many times the complaint is made *'They don't know how to write in complete sentences!'*

The complainers are talking about people like you. Do you know what they mean? Read this:

> Getting off the school bus, eating a leftover sandwich from his lunchbox.

This is not a complete sentence. Why not? What's wrong with it?

Well, a complete sentence will tell the reader who is doing something and when (past, present or future). This is achieved by including a **subject** and a **completed verb**.

Ask yourself who is doing this getting off the bus and eating? We don't know. Let's add a name:

> John, getting off the school bus, eating a leftover sandwich from his lunchbox.

It's still not complete, though, because John might be doing this getting off the bus and eating in the past or present or future.

Grammatically speaking, the words **getting** and **eating** are participles, which have been left 'hanging' without a subject (in this case John) and without more words to give the tense of the verb.

Here you can see how these sentences can be made complete.

> John **was** getting off the school bus, eating a leftover sandwich from his lunchbox. (past)

> John **is** getting off the school bus, eating a leftover sandwich from his lunchbox. (present)

> John **will be** getting off the school bus, eating a leftover sandwich from his lunchbox. (future)

Note that the additional words are assumed for the second part of the sentence. It would get a bit laborious to write:

> John was getting off the school bus and he was eating a leftover sandwich from his lunchbox.

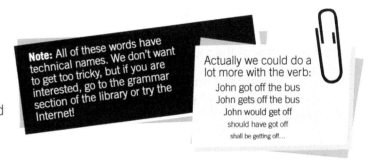

Note: All of these words have technical names. We don't want to get too tricky, but if you are interested, go to the grammar section of the library or try the Internet!

Actually we could do a lot more with the verb:
John got off the bus
John gets off the bus
John would get off
should have got off
shall be getting off…

Here's a straightforward exercise for you to complete to check that you can see how adding words to the …ing verb (the present participle) gives the time of the action (past, present or future).

Complete the grid

Present tense	Present continuous	Past tense	Past continuous	Future tense	Future continuous
I ask	I am asking	I asked	I was asking	I will ask	I will be asking
You describe			You were describing		
	He is managing				He will be managing
She hopes				She will hope	
They dance					

The past tense in English is interesting because it often does not follow this pattern of adding –ed to the core word as all the examples in column 3 above do.

Write the correct past tense in the space provided and add a sentence using the word correctly.

Verb	Incorrect past tense	Correct past tense	Sentence
write	writted	wrote	I wrote a letter to my friend.
eat	eated		
bring	bringed		
buy	buyed		
sleep	sleeped		
fight	fighted		
drive	drived		
sing	singed		

Try to make sure that all your sentences have a subject and at least one completed verb, unless you are using a minor sentence for deliberate effect! (*Examples:* Finished? Famished? Ready for dinner?)

ISBN 9780170195959

Week _____ Date for completion _____

Parent's sig. _____ Teacher's sig. _____

A film used for literary assessment can be studied according to its character, themes, events etc in just the same way as a novel or play can be. But unique to film are the issues surrounding *how* the director portrayed this information.

Most of you will be familiar with the shots and editing techniques directors use. In an essay devoted to film as text it is important that you refer to these techniques throughout your essay. You need to show your teacher that you are aware of the different ways a director gives his audience information in comparison to a writer. You must be able to identify techniques being used and explain what you think they contributed (or not) to the film.

This activity asks you to write a clear, detailed, thoughtful essay based on a film text you have studied in class. Complete the information in the box below before you begin.

Title of text: Director of text:

Note: The first bit of this activity may be best done as a class.

Let's take a look at the topic you have been given:

> **Explain how the beginning/opening of the text caught your attention and explain, with detailed reasons, how the director achieved this.**

Using a red or blue pen annotate the question:

- Put brackets around each part of the question
- Underline the key words in the question.

The opening scene is very important to a film. It sets up many of the details that will become important. It usually shows the setting and the main characters. It is also the scene that determines whether you, the viewer, are going to continue watching the film. Basically it needs to be good!

First things first: go back to your film and re-watch the opening scene/s. Decide exactly what you will refer to as the 'opening'. In most cases this will start from when the credits roll to the end of the first scene or sequence of short scenes.

You then need to systematically go through the scene several times taking notes as you do so. The **first** time you need to:

- Look carefully at what you see on the screen.
- Look at how the credits roll. Is there anything significant about them?
  The colour/font/appearance on and off the screen? What is the background?
- Look at the first shot. It is likely to be an establishing shot. What does it establish and why?
- Look at how the character/s is introduced. What type of shots/angles are used etc?
- Look at how they are dressed … what information is the costume giving you?
- Continue on looking at shots. Pick some that are significant. Perhaps a close-up, a soaring crane shot, a dissolve … look at why the director would have chosen to use them.

On the **second** time through concentrate on the soundtrack of the film. (In fact cover the screen or turn around so you are not looking at it.)

- Listen carefully to what you hear.
- What type of music is there? Orchestral? Modern? Is it haunting? Upbeat?
  What atmosphere is it setting up?
- Listen to the sounds the director and editors highlighted. Are they significant? Why?
- Listen to any dialogue. Why was the film opened with these lines? What do they tell us?

On your **third** watch:

- Put both of these together and check what you have written down.
  Fill in any details you may have missed.

Then … stop and think. What is attention grabbing about that opening? What made you take notice? What kept you watching? What questions were you left to wonder about?

Look through the notes that you have written down about the opening of your film. Go back to the question that you are answering and begin to decide how you will use the information you have gathered. **Think about:**

- what techniques you can comfortably talk about, expand, give examples of etc
- what order you are going to use them in making sure you answer both parts of the question.

You should now be ready to begin writing your essay.
Write the final copy of your essay in the back of this book.

If you need more guidance on writing a lilerary essay, refer to chapter 10 of your Year 10 *How to …* textbook.

Focus 2: Punctuation

Imagine that you are completing work experience with a city sign writer. One of your tasks is to proof the signs before they are painted. You quickly realise how important your job is! Correct the following signs. Most need the punctuation changing but some have spelling mistakes too.

BANANA'S FOR SALE

Joes Fish and Chips

**Mens' hairstylists.
No appointment necessary**

**PLEASE DON'T PARK HERE.
EXCESS REQUIRED AT ALL TIMES.**

Mrs S.T. Rapp
Principle

**DANGER!
Enter at you're own risk.**

NO UNDER-18S ALOUD

**christmas cakes
- our's are the best**

You can take all the photo's like these!
Complete one off out short courses and in three weeks, youll be taking shots like a pro!

**Security camera's
in operation**

**JONES AND SON'S
REMOVAL'S AND STORAGE**

**Bear Land.
For Sale**

The consumption of alcohol are not permitted on these premise

It can be fun to make a collection of your own from your neighbourhood.

ISBN 9780170195959

Week _____ Date for completion _____

Parent's sig. _____ Teacher's sig. _____

Focus 1: Visual close reading

Read this advertisement through carefully and highlight/annotate the layout elements of a visual text. Then look for as many examples of verbal techniques and visual techniques as you can possibly find. Make sure you do this tidily. Do not ruin your ability to see the overall image.

Layout
• Rule of thirds
• Balance (logos)

Visual techniques
• Contrast
• Logos
• Layout
• Frame/Box
• Font choice

Verbal techniques
• Personal pronouns
• Comparatives
• Contractions
• Use of the semicolon
• Use of dash
• Listing
• Minor sentence

Answer each question in as much detail as possible.

1 Describe the links between the visual image and the words in the advertisement.

_____

_____

_____

Always explain in as much detail as possible what the link between the words and the picture is. 'Headline', 'body copy' and 'image' should always be mentioned!

2 How does the small heading (top right) HELLO TOMORROW connect with the body copy? Quote from the text to support your answer.

_____

_____

_____

3. Is this an effective advertisement for Genesis Energy? Explain your answer in as much detail as possible.

_____

_____

_____

Tone is defined as the writer or speaker's attitude toward the subject or the intended audience. It can help if you think of the tone of a piece as the tone of voice in which it would be delivered.

To describe tone, imagine first of all someone reading aloud the passage– or extract– that you have been given. Ask yourself the question: in what tone of voice would it be read? Would it be:

SARCASTIC   humourous   scathing   angry   joyful

critical   serious   respectful   dramatic   reverent
    flippant

contemptuous   formal   ironic
    light-hearted   informal

… Or just … neutral (without a tone or point of view, if that is possible) …

At this stage, let's just think about how the way things are said can show tone.

1 Imagine the tone of voice that might be used to say each one of these sentences and write it down in the space provided.

a So, you put dishwashing liquid in the dishwasher – that was clever! _____

b I hate you! _____

c This is a really difficult decision for me. _____

d Let's get a pizza and fill our faces. _____

e Ladies and gentlemen, please take you seats. _____

2 Rewrite the following passage changing the highlighted words in order to change the tone from calm and friendly to angry and critical. You may add a few words if you wish.

'I cannot believe you want to go camping,' Brenda **said quietly**. 'You **don't like** sleeping anywhere but your own bed.'
Her brother **glanced** up at her from his book.
'Yes I do,' he **replied**. 'It's you who wants to stay home because you want to **stay** with your mates.'
Brenda **smiled** at him: '**OK**, you **tell** Dad that we'll go then.'

_____

_____

_____

_____

My Father Began as a God

My father began as a god,
full of heroic tales
of days when he was young.
His laws were as immutable
5   as if brought down from Sinai,
which indeed he thought they were.

He fearlessly lifted me to heaven
by a mere swing to his shoulder,
and made me a godling
10   by seating me astride
our milch-cow's back, and, too
upon the great white gobbler
of which others went in constant fear.

Strange then how he shrank and shrank
15   until by my time of adolescence
he had become a foolish small old man
with silly and outmoded views
of life and of morality.

Stranger still
20   that as I became older
his faults and his intolerances
scaled away into the past,
revealing virtues
such as honesty, generosity, integrity.

25   Strangest of all
how the deeper he recedes into the grave
the more I see myself
as just one more of all the little men
who creep through life
30   not knee-high to this long-dead god.

Ian Mudie

Do you remember the process to analysing a poem?

Step 1: Read – preferably aloud.
Step 2: Reread quietly,
          take in main ideas.
Step 3: Use a dictionary to help you
          with difficult vocabulary.
Step 4: Read again.
Step 5: Highlight poetic techniques.
Step 6: Discuss as a class/in pairs.
Step 7: Now you have all the
          information, reread
          the poem. Enjoy it!
Step 8: Answer any questions
          that follow.

You will need to look up the highlighted words in order to fully understand this poem.

- heroic
- immutable
- Sinai
- mere
- godling
- adolescence
- outmoded
- intolerances
- scaled away
- virtues
- integrity
- recedes

Locate the following techniques by underlining and annotating beside the poem.

- Simile
- Metaphor
- Alliteration
- Repetition

Answer each question in as much detail as possible.

1   What god-like qualities did the poet/narrator see in his father when he was a child? Support your answer with evidence from the text.

_____

_____

_____

2   Compare the attitude towards the father in the first two verses with those of the last three verses. What causes these changes? How does the poem's structure reflect these changes?

_____

_____

_____

ISBN 9780170195959

3 Explain in your own words the message or theme of this poem.

_____

_____

4 There are several references to features of religion in this poem. List them and explain why they might be used.

_____

_____

5 Think beyond the text. Do some thinking and some research. What is a god? What is a hero? Are they two different things?

_____

_____

_____

_____

_____

_____

_____

Olny srmat poelpe can raed tihs. I cdnuolt blveiee taht I cluod aulaclty uesdnatnrd waht I was rdanieg. The phaonmneal pweor of the hmuan mnid, aoccdrnig to a rscheearch at Cmabrigde Uinervtisy, it deosn't mttaer in waht oredr the ltteers in a wrod are, the olny iprmoatnt tihng is taht the frist and lsat ltteer be in the rghit pclae. The rset can be a taotl mses and you can sitll raed it wouthit a porbelm. Tihs is bcuseae the huamn mnid deos not raed ervey lteter by istlef, but the wrod as a wlohe. Amzanig huh? yaeh and I awlyas tghuhot slpeling was ipmorantt!

Which is probably not the best way to introduce:

Trouble is, all those words above have the right letters in them, so whoever wrote them needed to know the correct letters to use before he or she mixed them up.

So: here is a list of words we often see spelt incorrectly. Do you know them all? Test yourself by getting someone to read them out, while you try to write them down correctly.

address	grown	momentary	shown	yourselves
because	hopeful	noise	typical	zoology
character	imagine	onomatopoeia	understandable	
describe	journey	practice/practise	victorious	
exaggerate	knowledge	quotation	weight	
flown	literature	reputation	example	

Keep a list here of the words that have been corrected in your schoolwork (not just in English, but in Geography, Science, and History etc too). Make sure you never make the same mistake twice!

Words I misspell frequently...

_____ _____ _____ _____

_____ _____ _____ _____

_____ _____ _____ _____

ISBN 9780170195959

Structuring your essay

A formal essay needs a formal structure. Your writing will be more authoritative and convincing if it is well arranged. Here is a reminder of a simple structure that you will find easy to follow when you are writing a formal essay.

- state the topic
- state your point of view (which side of the topic you are arguing)
- give the three main ideas you will use
- make this paragraph interesting and convincing – believe in yourself!

- have no fewer than three ideas in three separate paragraphs.

- a topic sentence that states the idea
- an explanation saying in more detail what you meant in your topic sentence
- evidence that supports your explanation with an effective example, anecdote, statistic, quotation …
- a concluding connection to the topic.

If you need more guidance on writing a formal essay, refer to chapter 7 of your Year 10 *How to …* textbook.

Tricks of the trade:
- use a dictionary
- use a thesaurus
- use a spell checker (machine and person)
- use an editor
- and for those elusive ideas – the brainstorm!

These are the essentials:
- correct spelling
- correct paragraphing
- correct use of punctuation
- correct sentence structure.

And the ideals:
- expressive vocabulary
- good organisation or structure
- great ideas

Don't forget:
Try to imagine your essay is the last thing that the person making the final decision on your issue will read and it should therefore persuade them to agree with your opinion.

Your task is to write a formal essay on the topic:

Winning is everything.

Below is a collection of points that have been compiled to help you with your initial thinking and planning. Of course you may like to add to your information by talking to your parents, siblings and grandparents, by looking on the Internet, in the library etc.

- Who cares if athletes lose? Doing their best is what counts.
- It is not the winning but the participation and good spirit that counts.
- Stop the nit picking and blame shifting when we lose.
- Great when we win a medal. Silver and bronze are good too.
- It's nice to see everyone have a go.
- Losing is bad.
- To participate is to win.
- I enjoy watching all sports.
- I cheer everyone on. I don't care who wins. Good competition is great, especially if the outcome between places is close.
- Be proud of all our athletes whether they win or lose!
- Pressure on our athletes to succeed.
- Bad example set for children and young people.
- Encouraging participation to fight obesity.
- Screaming and cheering at the top of our lungs.
- 'Kiwi Sports' too PC, there were no winners or losers – useless preparation for the Commonweath Games or the Olympics.
- Stop trying to protect children from reality.
- There are winners and losers in real life.
- Could our athletes' 'lack of toughness' be the result of years of the namby-pamby way sport is treated in schools?

Write the final copy of your essay in the back of this book.

ISBN 9780170195959

Focus 2: Research

Use a search engine to find the lyrics to the song 'Big Yellow Taxi'. While you are there do some research into the history of the song. If your computer has the capabilities listen to the song or search through your parents' music collection to find it!

List the steps you took to locate the lyrics and supporting information in detail. Your teacher should be able to follow your steps and end up at exactly the same site you did!

> Lyrics are a type of poem. Listening to them being sung is a very pleasurable alternative to reading and rereading them. See if you can find one of the versions of this song to listen to.

Research steps

Step 1 _____

Step 2 _____

Step 3 _____

Step 4 _____

Step 5 _____

Step 6 _____

Step 7 _____

Either print or copy out the lyrics of the song and glue it to the top of this page.

Now answer each question in as much detail as possible.

1   The song is about regret. The first three verses describe three kinds of things the writer believes the modern world is losing. What are those things?

   a _____

    _____

   b _____

    _____

   c _____

    _____

2   Connect each of these three things to where you live. Explain how the sentiment is or is not relevant for your world.

   a _____

    _____

   b _____

    _____

   c _____

    _____

3   Who do you think is the 'they' that the song keeps referring to?

   _____

4   The refrain says:

> Don't it always seem to go
> That you don't know what you've got 'til it's gone

What does this mean?

   _____

   _____

5   When this song was written it was part of a protest movement. Go to the Internet or to the library and find out what Joni Mitchell herself was protesting about.

ISBN 9780170195959

Week _____ Date for completion _____

Parent's sig. _____ Teacher's sig. _____

Focus 1: Visual close-reading

If you look carefully at this visual text you will notice that there is very little 'written' on it. Its effectiveness comes from the image itself.

Read and examine the advertisement carefully and highlight/annotate the layout elements of a visual text.

Then look for as many examples of verbal techniques and visual techniques as you can possibly find. Make sure you do this tidily. Do not ruin your ability to see the overall image.

Layout
- Rule of thirds
- Balance

Verbal
- Personal pronouns
- Contractions
- Alliteration
- Repetition
- Comparative adjective

Visual
- Contrast
- DVF
- Background
- Style of font
- Use of upper case lettering
- Logos
- Punctuation

ISBN 9780170195959

Answer each question in as much detail as possible.

1 What is the visual text promoting? _____

2 Where is Aoraki Polytechnic? _____

3 Why would the designer have chosen dark brown as the background for the top and bottom thirds?

_____

4 How do the verbal and visual features of this advertisement combine?

_____

_____

_____

_____

_____

It is not our normal practice to give you 'games' but we decided … just this once … that we would loosen up and give you something 'fun'.

Eliminate words in the table according to the instructions. When you have finished, the words that remain in the table will spell out a phrase when you read them from left to right, top to bottom.

DOOR	LEAVES	DON'T	QUICK
PUT	SPOON	CORGI	SLATE
RUN	SUNNY	BAKER	ALL
CARAMEL	YOUR	SPEEDY	WINDOW
EGGS	FARMER	WALL	LADLE
LEAST	SEE	IN	RAINY
FAST	TOFFEE	SEEDS	ONE
COLLIE	BASKET	TONGS	ACTOR

1 Eliminate kitchen utensils in rows 2,5 and 8
2 Eliminate words that mean the opposite of 'slow' in columns A, C and D
3 Eliminate verbs in rows 3 and 6
4 Eliminate words relating to plants in columns B and C
5 Eliminate occupations in rows 3, 5 and 8
6 Eliminate words that form an anagram of 'stale' in columns A and D
7 Eliminate sweet treats in rows 4 and 7
8 Eliminate parts of a house in columns A, C and D
9 Eliminate weather-related words in rows 3 and 6
10 Eliminate dogs in columns A and C

ANSWER: _____

Below is a list of metaphors that are all for the same object. You know that a metaphor is where you say something is something else. Your task is to discover what object these metaphors connect to. Look carefully at the image each of these creates. Create the picture in your mind. What do they all have in common?

1 The hut stands by itself beneath the palms.
2 Out of their bottle the green genie came.
3 A vine has climbed the other side of the wall.
4 The sea is sprouting upward out of the rocks.
5 These lozenges are nailed up lattices.
6 The owl sits humped. It has a hundred eyes.
7 This is how yesterday's volcano looks.
8 The coconut and cockerel in one.

Can you work out what the object is? It will take a bit of lateral thinking … and yes, it will get quite frustrating. You might need to enlist the help of your parents!

Hey teachers – there might have to be a chocolate bar up for whoever gets this one!

OBJECT: _____

ISBN 9780170195959

UNIT 19

Week _____ Date for completion _____

Parent's sig. _____ Teacher's sig. _____

HINT FOR SUCCESS
The Internet has a wealth of information but be selective! Make sure you use reputable sites and always write down where you got your information from.

This is the first part of a newspaper feature article.

Thawing ice heats debate on sovereignty

Vanishing Arctic cover reveals a very different Greenland with new political ambitions, writes **Daniel Howden**

Climbing out of Ilulissat, past the wooden houses built to withstand the arctic cold, the howls of the sled dogs form a sad chorus. Up on the plateau in clear view of the glacier, thousands of them prowl among disused sleds, chained to the tundra in packs waiting for a winter that no longer comes.

Each spring the inhabitants of this northern outpost, more than 180 km inside the Arctic Circle, march through the darkness along this route to the edge of the ice fjord to greet the first light of the year. On that morning the sun appears for twenty minutes. It is one of the few remaining constants for Greenlanders in a world that has otherwise changed beyond comprehension in the last decade.

The Jacobshaven glacier still calves icebergs larger than supertankers into the vast Disko Bay but the ice sheet that once crept south each year to provide the dog-sledders with frozen hunting ground is now an infrequent visitor. The glacier itself is accelerating into the sea at a rate by now visible to the naked eye.

A very different Greenland is emerging from underneath the thawing ice. The largest and most northerly island in the world is home to a tiny population of just 56,000. Most of its interior is weighed down by an immense ice cap, the glacial fingers of which provide the spectacle of Greenland's ice-fjords. During the winter the polar sea ice stretches south shutting off sea routes to the settlements that dot its jagged coastline.

This harsh landscape was where Aleqa Hammond grew up in a family of hunters. Now the Foreign Minister of Greenland's home rule Government, she is also one of the chief advocates of this unique country's bid for independence. For centuries under the sway of Norway, it is now a self-governing province of Denmark that had been thought to be too weak economically to stand on its own but that, she claims, is about to change.

"The economic independence of Greenland is within range," she told participants at the Religion Science and the Environment symposium.

Greenland depends on a $81.7 million annual grant from Copenhagen but the vast mineral wealth believed to be lying beneath the seabed could dwarf that income if it could be verified and exploited.

Her administration is already in talks with nine multinationals who want oil exploration licences. And Greenland's politicians talk like true believers in the coming bonanza. "In this bay at the next fjord you can touch the oil," says Ms Hammond…

Answer each question in as much detail as possible.

On the surface

1 Where is Ilulissat? How long is its shortest day? _____

_____

2 What is Greenland's national status? _____

_____

3 How many people live in Greenland? Why does the writer mention this? _____

_____

Technical

4 The headline of the article uses an **oxymoron** (figure of speech that puts together two words of opposite meaning). Identify and explain its use. _____

_____

5 The word *Arctic* (Arctic Circle) is also written as *arctic* (arctic cold). Why the difference? _____

_____

_____

6 What language technique is used to describe the formation of icebergs? Why? _____

_____

_____

7 The writer uses a cliché, 'to the naked eye'. What does this phrase mean?

_____

_____

ISBN 9780170195959

Search and think

8 Why does the writer begin his article with a description of dogs? _____

_____

_____

9 The writer says the world has 'changed beyond comprehension in the last decade'. What has changed in Greenland? Look at both negatives and positives. _____

_____

_____

_____

_____

_____

You might also examine the emotive language, alliteration and metaphor.

Focus 2: Apostrophes

A Easy: used in contractions to show where letters are missing.

Write the full version of these contractions:

1 Who's (_____ _____) the fastest runner?

2 Jane is, she's (_____ _____) won every race this term.

3 I thought Marama was the fastest but she didn't (_____ _____) even come third.

4 She won't (_____ _____) practise enough; she'll (_____ _____) be fastest when she does.

B Fairly easy: showing possession by adding 's to a singular noun.

Turn these phrases into ones using a possessive apostrophe – copy the example.

Example: The roof of the house -> The house's roof

1 The socks of John   -> _____

2 The schoolbag of Jill   -> _____

3 The bicycle of the child -> _____

4 Branches of a tree   -> _____

C A bit trickier: when the noun is plural (add 's) and/or ends in s (add ')

Choose the correct word from the two choices given.

1 All the boys'/boy's socks were stolen from the changing rooms

2 The children's/childrens' schoolbags were all pink.

3 Ten bikes'/bike's handlebars leant against the shed wall.

4 Several tree's/trees' branches were lopped by the arborist.

D The trickiest little word: It's or its?

Use **it's** ONLY when you could expand the contraction to **it is** or **it has**.

Put the correct version in the space provided:

1 A dog's bark is worse than _____ bite.

2 _____ going to be a fine day today.

3 _____ been fine all this week.

4 The possum caught _____ leg in the trap.

5 Our car is an old heap; _____ going to fall apart any day now.

And our perennial advice 'If in doubt, leave it out!' A sprinkling of misplaced apostrophes looks so much worse than the occasional omission of one.

UNIT 20

Week _____ Date for completion _____

Parent's sig. _____ Teacher's sig. _____

HINT FOR SUCCESS
Make sure you are using appropriate language choices for your audience. Think: who am I speaking to?

Imagine your local beach (or riverside) has been damaged by pollution of some sort. You are a local journalist and have researched this story. Write your article.

Aim to write at least 300 words.

Here is the brainstorm of a student to help you with ideas.
You may add your own ideas relating to your part of the country.
You may need to do a little research.
You don't have to use everything mentioned in the brainstorm.

If you need more guidance on writing a newspaper article, refer to chapter 9 of your Year 10 *How to ...* textbook.

Damage is done by vehicles

Take your rubbish home

Penguins damaged, fairy terns??

Plastic things that don't break down – inorganic?

Mammals , birds eat plastic then die

Animals and fish can get tangled up in lines, nets

Seals, dolphins, whales – all marine mammals

Don't catch little fish, fish need to breed

Vehicles only for towing boats and carrying fishing gear

wildlife in trouble = people in trouble

Nesting birds hurt/killed

Not all teenagers are hoons

Dogs not on leads are a nuisance

who looks after the beaches?

Don't bother dolphins and whales and mothers with babies when you're swimming

4WDS cause problems

Boats shouldn't dump effluent

Quad bikes

Water pollution

Remember that:

- When something is enclosed within brackets, it is usually an explanation, an aside or some additional information.
- If you take away the words in parenthesis, the rest of the sentence should still make complete sense.
- If the material enclosed falls at the end of a sentence, the full stop is placed outside the closing parenthesis.

1   Fill in each gap in the postcards below with the appropriate aside.

ISBN 9780170195959

Dear Mum and Dad (_____)

I'm having a great time (_____

_____) with Jess's family. Th

bay is amazing (_____;

and we've got a fabulous tent. I'm going diving

tomorrow (_____) with

Jess's brother (_____).

Don't worry, I've done the training!

Love Riley

Asides: white sand, blue water etc etc/ and Charlie, if I must/he's 30 and dives for a living/weather permitting/missing you all of course!

Asides: sore muscles/good grief/ drew the short straw/but freezing/ way worse than Mum!

Hey Mia

It's choice here (_____).

We're skiing every day (_____)

and dancing every night. I'm sharing a room with

Grace (_____) and she's

sooo untidy (_____).

Can't wait for tomorrow night when there's a bbq

(_____) out in the snow!

See ya, Greer

2   The writers of these notes did not know how to use brackets. Rewrite them, using brackets accurately.

Mum and (Dad, if you're home),

I am sorry about the mess in the living room. Or should I call it (the disaster area?)
Paul and I had a few people well, (maybe more than just a few over last night) and we
haven't had a chance to clean …

Dear Amy

… There is no homework (for Geography) miracle of miracles … Christy

ISBN 9780170195959

Week _____ Date for completion _____

Parent's sig. _____ Teacher's sig. _____

Focus 1: Understanding poetry

Poetry can be the most demanding sort of writing to understand. Take your time. Use your imagination. You can cope – we have faith in you.

Do you remember the process for analysing a poem?

Step 1: Read – preferably aloud.

Step 2: Reread quietly, take in main ideas.

Step 3: Use a dictionary to help you with difficult vocabulary.

Step 4: Read again.

Step 5: Highlight poetic techniques.

Step 6: Discuss as a class/in pairs.

Step 7: Now you have all the information, reread the poem. Enjoy it!

Step 8: Answer any questions that follow.

You will need to look up the highlighted words in order to fully understand this poem.

• truculent
• derelict
• phantoms
• ghastly
• gouged
• intermittently
• morse
• brooding
• fate

Locate the following techniques by underlining and annotating beside the poem.

• Onomatopoeia
• Personification (x 3)
• Alliteration (x 2)

August, Ohakune

All night in winter the dogs howled
Up the hill in the mad woman's house –
she had forty living inside,
half-starved, truculent, snarling

5   at all who came; but only kids
would creep along the derelict track:
half choked with fear they stalked phantoms,
found their nightmare, an ancient stag,
eyeless, ghastly holes gouged

10 by rats, above the blackened door.
They smothered screams – and went back,
In daylight only....
                    Further off we could hear the river
Intermittently tapping its menacing morse
And the morepork call through the dark;

15 At last the frost hunted us in
To take shelter in cold uneasy sleep.

Over all was the mountain, Snow Queen
Of an old tale, brilliant and deadly, brooding
On the fate of frozen villages.

Lauris Edmond

1   In each verse the poet describes a threat. Explain these threats in your own words.

First _____

_____

Second _____

_____

Third _____

_____

2   How does the poet emphasise the aggression of the dogs? _____

_____

3   Explain the effect of the use of personification in the poem. _____

_____

_____

_____

Well, here we are nearly at the end of the book. Most of you will have worked through the Year 9 workbook and now the Year 10 workbook. But the question is, how much have we actually managed to instil inside your head?

At this point you are probably starting to think about next year and its rather daunting external examinations. We've decided to take some time to remind you how much you actually know already.

The following activity will send you off through both this workbook and the accompanying textbook in order to find the answers. We would like to suggest that you:

- Begin by using a pencil and doing as much as you can using what you already know.
- Then go back through this book, the textbook, the library, the Internet, basically wherever you can to check your answers and fill in any gaps.

Good luck!

Term	Definition	Why it is used
Alliteration		
Metaphor		
Simile		
Personification		
Repetition		
Onomatopoeia		
Rhyme		
Pun		
Euphemism		
Imagery		
Pronoun		
Brackets		
Ellipsis		
Balance		
Contrast		
Empty space		
Symbol		
Emotive language		
Rhetorical question		
Listing		

Week _____ Date for completion _____

Parent's sig. _____ Teacher's sig. _____

Cemetery Path

Leonard Q. Ross

Ivan was a timid little man – so timid that the villagers called him 'Pigeon' or mocked him with the title 'Ivan the Terrible'. Every night Ivan stopped at a saloon on the edge of the village cemetery. Ivan never crossed the cemetery to get to his lonely shack on the other side. The path through the cemetery would save him many minutes but Ivan had never taken it – not even in the full light of the moon.

Late one winter's night, when a bitter wind and snow beat against the saloon, the customers took up their familiar mockery of Ivan. His mild protests only fed their taunts, and they laughed when a young Cossack lieutenant flung a challenge at their quarry. 'You are a pigeon, Ivan. A rabbit. A coward. You'll walk around the cemetery in this dreadful cold, to get home, but you dare not across the cemetery.'

Ivan murmured. 'The cemetery – it is nothing to cross, Lieutenant. I am not afraid. The cemetery is nothing but earth.'

The lieutenant cried, 'A challenge, then! Cross the cemetery tonight, now, and I'll give you five gold roubles – five gold roubles!'

Perhaps it was the vodka. Perhaps it was the temptation of the five gold roubles. No one ever knew why Ivan, moistening his lips, blurted: 'All right, Lieutenant, I'll cross the cemetery!'

As the saloon echoed with the villagers' derision and disbelief, the lieutenant winked to the others and unbuckled his saber. 'Here, Ivan. Prove yourself. When you get to the very centre of the cemetery, in front of the biggest tomb, stick my sabre into the ground! In the morning we shall go there. And if the saber is in the ground – five gold roubles to you!'

Slowly Ivan took the saber. The villagers drank a toast: 'To Ivan the Hero! Ivan the Terrible!' They roared with laughter.

The wind howled around Ivan as he closed the door of the saloon behind him. The cold was as sharp as a butcher's knife. He buttoned his long coat and crossed the road. He could hear the lieutenant's voice, louder than the rest, calling after him, 'Five gold roubles, little pigeon! Five roubles – if you live!'

Ivan strode to the cemetery gates, and hesitated, and pushed the gate open.

He walked fast. 'Earth, it's just earth … like any other earth.' But the darkness was a massive dread. 'Five gold roubles …' The wind was savage and the saber was like ice in his hands. Ivan shivered under the long, thick coat and broke into a limping run.

He recognised the large tomb. No one could miss that large edifice. Ivan must have sobbed – but that was drowned in the wind. And Ivan kneeled, cold and terrified, and in a frenzy or fear drove the saber into the hard ground. It was hard to do, but he beat it down into the hard earth with his fist, down to the very hilt. It was done! The cemetery … the challenge … five roubles … five gold roubles!

Ivan started to rise from his knees. But something gripped him in an unyielding, implacable hold. Ivan swore and tugged and lurched and pulled – gasping in his panic, sweating despite the knife-edged cold, shaken by fear. But something held Ivan. He cried out in terror against the unseen imprisonment, and he tried to rise, using all his strength. But he could not rise.

They found Ivan, the next morning, on the ground right in front of the great tomb that was in the very centre of the cemetery. His face was not that of a frozen man, but of a man slain by some nameless horror. And the lieutenant's saber was in the ground where Ivan had pounded it – through the dragging folds of his long and shabby coat.

ISBN 9780170195959

1 Describe the setting: the place and the time in which the story takes place. Give evidence to support your answer. _____

_____

2 Why has the author chosen a cold winter's night on which to set his story? _____

_____

3 What are the differences between Ivan and the lieutenant? _____

_____

4 How does the reader know that Ivan is afraid when he accepts the challenge? _____

_____

5 How is the lieutenant's contempt for Ivan shown to the reader? _____

_____

6 Why does the lieutenant make the challenge? Give detail from the passage. _____

_____

7 What is Ivan's motive for accepting the challenge? What are his fears? _____

_____

8 How does Ivan try to build his courage? _____

_____

9 Which detail shows that Ivan is under great stress? _____

_____

10 What is the climactic point of the story? _____

_____

1 The writer creates a winter scene very effectively. List four emotive words or phrases that help to establish the cruel environment. _____

_____

_____

2 How does the author create an atmosphere of panic in paragraphs 7 and 8? _____

_____

_____

ISBN 9780170195959

1 Ivan is a character in a conflict situation. With whom is he in conflict? Hint; think about both external and internal conflict.

_____

_____

2 Circle the words you think best describe Ivan's personality.

lonely	happy	greedy	wealthy
scared	bitter	poor	brave

Choose THREE and find a quotation that backs up each one.

a _____

_____

_____

b _____

_____

_____

c _____

_____

_____

Answer one of the questions below in a paragraph of about 70 words.

1 Is this short story a comedy or a tragedy? Or both? Explain your reasons for your answer.

OR

2 How does this short story illustrate the way greed leads people into making poor decisions? Is this an issue in your world?

_____

_____

_____

_____

_____

_____

_____

_____

_____

_____

_____

_____

_____

_____

_____

ISBN 9780170195959

1   Give the story a positive end for Ivan by rewriting the end of the story from the line 'Ivan started to rise from his knees …'.

OR

2   Write a modern day version of the same story.

Week _____ Date for completion _____

Parent's sig. _____ Teacher's sig. _____

Answer these questions, before we begin:

What language do people who live in Spain speak? _____

What language do people who live in Sweden speak? _____

What language do people who live in China speak? _____

What language do people who live in Korea speak? _____

What language do people who live in Germany speak? _____

What language do people who live in Italy speak? _____

So why don't people in New Zealand speak New Zealandish? Or Aotearoan? And why do people who live in the United States of America, and Canada, and Australia have English as their first language as we do here in New Zealand? And why do so many people in China and India and Europe have English as their second language?

People from England speak English. But so do people from Scotland, Wales and Northern Ireland. These countries make up the United Kingdom. In 1840, these islands, which we call New Zealand, became a colony of the British Empire when the representative of the British monarch, Queen Victoria, signed a Treaty with some Maori chiefs. You will have heard of the place where it was signed – Waitangi.

It just so happened that New Zealand joined a group of countries where English was spoken and English over the next few decades up to the present became the lingua franca, the common tongue, of much of the western world because it was the language of the country that became all powerful – the United States of America.

Many of the English speaking settlers who came to New Zealand were of Scottish, Irish or urban working class English backgrounds. Many Australian settlers, convicts or free people were of similar background. The accents are similar. In New Zealand we can tell the difference between an Australian and a New Zealander but often people from Britain or from the United States cannot.

What makes New Zealand English distinct – apart from the accent – are the words that have entered the language here and nowhere else. Naturally the main contributor is Maori. The settlers adopted Maori names for local trees, flowers and birds. *Kauri, toi-toi, weka*, are all Maori words which we use in New Zealand English. *Kete* meaning basket was kit for a while but we are used to the word kete itself now. Grandparents tickle babies and use the word *puku* for tummy. Most of us, even if we do not speak Maori, know the meaning of lots of Maori words and do not need to have them translated.

Do you know the English word for these words and phrases?

haere mai   **haere ra**

hangi   **hui**

hongi   **ka pai**

kaumatua

kaupapa

kei te pehea koe?

kete

mere

marae

mokopuna

pa

piupiu

poi

porangi

puku

tangi

taniwha

taonga

tapu

whare

whare kai

Your school may have a motto in Maori. You can all sing the New Zealand National Anthem in Maori – your parents, if they are not Maori, would probably not have been able to do so when they were young. The times, they are a'changin'.

Write down the first verse of the New Zealand national anthem, first the Maori version then the English one.

Māori version

E Ihoa Atuā

English version

God of Nations at thy feet

ISBN 9780170195959

In earlier times the rural landscape and farming in particular provided lots of words and phrases special to New Zealand. *'Rattle your dags,'* is not a phrase you will find used much in England!

Here are some interesting New Zealand words and phrases. Write what you think each one means and then check your answers with your teacher.

A and P show

Bach

Biddy-bid

Boohai

Box of birds

Captain Cooker

Up Central

Colonial goose

Dog tucker

Eskimo pie

Get in behind

FOB

Gentle Annie

Gib board

Hospital pass

Kilikiti

King country

Kit

Last shower

Lemon squeezer

Maimai

Pakeha

Palagi

Smoko

Stairdancer

Tiki tour

Plastic tiki

Sweet as/ She'll be sweet

Taranaki gate

The word *bush* with the meaning of uncleared land, scrub, or forest has lots of compounds created from it. Use a good New Zealand dictionary and find the meaning of these words. Add three more yourself.

bush lawyer

bush-clad

bush telegraph

1

2

3

ISBN 9780170195959

Many people today think that New Zealand is losing its distinct features under an onslaught of North American culture, primarily through television, the Internet and Hollywood. We are gradually choosing the American word in favour of the British one.

Do you go to the movies or to the cinema? _____

Do you wear sneakers or plimsolls? _____

Does your baby sister have a nappy or a diaper? _____

Are your clothes in a wardrobe or a closet? _____

Does your Dad fill the car with petrol or gas? _____

We're pretty close to Australia but even there, there are differences.

Pair up the Australian and New Zealand words

thong	bull bar
Icy pole	dairy
durex	sheep
snags	bangers (sausages)
cossie	sarnie
esky	jandal
jumbuck	chillibin
milk bar	sellotape
roo bar	ice block
sanger	togs

Another consequence of this accident by which we speak English in New Zealand is to make us lazy. Many New Zealanders speak only English. Most of us do not learn a second language. If you have another language at home, whether it is Maori, Chinese, Korean, Spanish or whatever … you are fortunate!

ISBN 9780170195959

Week _____ Date for completion _____

Parent's sig. _____ Teacher's sig. _____

Your task is to produce a piece of descriptive writing (about 300 words) which uses figures of speech and careful planning to reach an unexpected end.

This writing task is aimed at improving the following things:

- your descriptive writing, particularly creating an atmosphere
- your ability to plan, because the surprise ending must be known first and planned towards
- your use of figures of speech such as simile and personification
- having some fun!

To do this you will have to utilise all you have learnt about:

- adjectives and adverbs
- emotive language.

You will be assessed on:

- imaginative and interesting writing
- fluent, controlled, structured writing
- careful spelling, word usage and punctuation
- writing that is clearly related to the topic.

Have a look at how others have created successful suspense stories

Tomorrow …

Tomorrow would be a whole new day, if only it would come, she thought to herself. She sat staring at the fading sunset. She was frightened; something or someone was watching her and she didn't know what to do. She wished she could just wake up and find it was tomorrow.

As she sat, the Indians crept upon her. They enclosed her. They were skilful and silent like leopards. Suddenly, without warning, their leader let out an ear piercing war cry and lunged forward. Frightened for her life she began to run. She ran as fast as she could, faster than the wind but still they managed to keep up. They followed her everywhere she went. Finally she was out of breath and could run no more. Frantically she searched for a place to hide. Quickly she climbed into a small space hoping they wouldn't find her. The Indians ran right past her and she let out a sign of relief.

Unfortunately they had good hearing; they heard her and came running back. She didn't know what to do. They were so close she could see the evil glints in their eyes. It was as though they could smell her fear. They smiled wickedly at each other. They were all around her, so close she could feel their warm breath on her neck. Roughly they grabbed her and dragged her back towards their hut. She dared not think about what they might do to her. Frantically she began kicking and screaming, she bit and scratched to no avail. Their iron-like grips prevented her from escaping.

Finally they reached the hut. The fearsome Indians tied her to the stake. They began circling her like a pack of vultures. One of them started chanting and the others followed suit. Gradually the changing became more intense, the noise reverberating in her ears like the church bells striking twelve. Suddenly without warning the chanting stopped. United as one, the Indians lifted their spears. She

ISBN 9780170195959

finally understood, the end was near, although she had no idea what she had done to them. She closed her eyes and prayed, the Indians took aim …

At the same moment she heard a car pull into the driveway. Quickly, the kids untied her and ran off to bed. She sighed as another evening of babysitting finished. She went home so tomorrow would come.

She clutched the fur collar to her throat …

She clutched the fur collar to her throat, darting her head around, anxiously trying to spot her stalker. It was a chilly night and she was glad she had had the common sense to bring her fur-lined overcoat with her. There it was again! A quiet rustling in the bushes as though something was trying to inconspicuously creep through them.

Holding her overcoat even tighter to her small frame, she reached for something, anything to protect herself with. Grasping a small tree branch in her left hand for protection she carefully advanced towards the bushes.

She heard a faint sound of a car driving away in the distance, but all around was the cold, clammy darkness of the night. Like some great creature which had swallowed her up, night time had fallen before she could make her way back home from her evening walk in the park.

And now someone or something was creeping stealthily through the bushes, approaching her. Just the thought of what horror might lay behind those looming branches sent a tingle of fear up her spine. 'W-who's there?' she called in a whisper muffled by fear. There was no answer, but again the bush rustled, and then she heard it coming closer and closer, nearer and nearer.

She turned in a panic to escape, letting loose a sob from her quivering mouth. Away from the bush she ran, hurling away her wooden weapon which she had hoped would protect her. Then she tripped over something on the ground and she collapsed in a panicking flurry. Her attacker was on her back, clawing at her and she felt something wet on her face.

Opening one of her eyes, she gazed up into the face of her stalker. Relief overcame her and she sat up laughing and hugged him. 'Ben,' she said. 'What a bad dog you are to follow me on my walk, you know you're not allowed to.'

Think about these factors:
- the fact that the real situation was not revealed until the end
- the fact that the writer must have planned the story in reverse,
  deciding on the surprise ending and writing towards it
- the 'key sentence', that tells you what the paragraph is about,
  is usually found at the beginning a paragraph … where it is in these examples?
- the key to fooling the reader is creating a realistic atmosphere
- the variety of vocabulary. Reread each story highlighting effective adjectives,
  adverbs and verbs as you go
- the use of similes to help build the description.

Choose one of the previous stories and annotate/highlight it using these bullet points (above).

Brainstorm

Take 5 minutes to brainstorm as many possible topics for a similar story as you can. Note: Journeys are always a good topic – e.g. getting from A to B, walking to the loo in the middle of the night! Remember the idea of a suspense story is the 'suspense'. Don't tell your friends what you are working on or it will ruin the surprise!

ISBN 9780170195959

Write a draft

Using the ideas you have gained from your brainstorm, draft a piece of writing of your own.

Craft your writing

Use the following checklist to make sure you have done everything.

◯ I have an introduction that creates interest and makes my audience want to read on.

◯ I have used a thesaurus to improve the variety of my vocabulary.

◯ I have read my essay aloud and corrected any errors I could hear.

◯ I have checked my spelling with a dictionary.

◯ I have checked that all my sentences start with a capital letter and end in a full stop.

◯ I have checked that I have used paragraphs to show development and change.

Let others read it and see if they are surprised.

Publication

Give your story a title and copy it onto page 71.

Here is a story that we thought you might enjoy reading. The author uses a similar style as you have just worked with. Although it is perhaps less obvious in its climatic build and suspense there is still an unexpected twist and realisation built into the end. Having learnt to use the style maybe you can use elements of it in your next piece of creative writing.

Red
By Bonnie Isiah

Her porcelain-white face showed no emotion. I studied her as she stepped out into the gale and proceeded forward. Drops of mercury fell from the sky and disrupted her clean image. The rain was colder than the devils' heart. I watched, satisfied, as her auburn curls began to expand in a grayed mess. Automatically her hands were drawn like magnets to her unkempt hair and were hurriedly trying to tame the frizz. I smirked as her chipped crimson talons tugged at her now imperfect image. Typically, as she was passing a window, she studied herself in the reflection. There's a reason vanity's a sin, I thought.

She stumbled senselessly in ebony stilettos, trying to dismiss the discomfort she was experiencing. As she marched, the daggers on her feet repeatedly stabbed the ground. She was the symbolic, desirable, pretty thoughtless ditz; the girl who everyone was envious of appearance-wise. It's well known that intelligence and intellect are the key to advancement in life, earning you respect and surpassing other qualities, but I believe that is all a myth.

I observed the girl snap at a vulnerable naïve boy of elementary age for colliding with her accidentally. It infuriated me to witness that he immediately apologized, his eyes wide in awe due to her surreal beauty. She turned abruptly, her scarlet curls showering the boy with icy drops of water. Her vermillion locks seemed aflame and reflected her fiery personality. The dull thud, thud, thud, of her high-heels echoed throughout the chamber. Her stilettos pierced the earth's skin with each movement. She seemed so dominating, so fierce. I longed to be like her. Beauty does get you somewhere in this unfair, tainted world, and I didn't care. It didn't matter to me that intelligence was no longer admired. After all, what could I do about it?

Suddenly she turned to face me, and her cherry lips curved upwards. She hurried towards me, wielding a black leather handbag on one shoulder which weighed her down. Her torso was an unbalanced see-saw. As she advanced, her footsteps were beating to the uneven rhythm of a heart. Thump-thump. Thump-thump. The faster she went the more she punctured the ground.

She looked up. The shimmer in her soft hazel eyes revealed to me that she was still the same person I knew and envied.

'Hey sis!' she beamed. 'God I'm sooo stupid; I forgot what time to meet! Luckily one of us has brains in the family, huh?' She nudged me, chuckling. 'Lucky you.' she murmured, and at that moment I realized that the connection to envy was reversed, symmetrical: we both admired and wanted to be each other.

ISBN 9780170195959

Use this page to write the final copy of your suspense story.

ISBN 9780170195959

UNIT 25 (EXTENDED)

Week _____ Date for completion _____

Parent's sig. _____ Teacher's sig. _____

We have included a typical Year 10 end-of-year assessment from a typical New Zealand school. Use it to help you prepare for your final examination. You may choose to sit this in 3 hours or you may choose to spread it over several days. We are sure that your teacher will be more than happy to mark any work that you complete.

Year Ten English Exam

**Time allowed: 3 hours
(1 hour per section)**

Section 1: Close reading of unfamiliar texts
Section 2: Response to texts
Section 3: Formal writing

Read the extracts and answer the questions which follow.

Section 1a: Poetic text

Read the following poem and answer all the questions that follow:

Jaguar

Sleek-bodied,
With gleaming flanks.
Nature's latest model.
Caught in the rays of the afternoon's dying sun
For a brief moment,   5
The light shining and rippling down the long smooth side.
There she stands,
Purring gently,
Engine ticking over.

Then, deftly, gracefully,   10
She moves into first gear:
Slides forward,
Gathers speed:
Until with full throttle open
She utters her full-throated roar,   15
And unleashed
Leaps across the intersection-
Steel-muscled acrobat
Arching through the dark.

But suddenly the light thins sharply.   20
She starts to brake,
Veers swiftly to the left,
Decelerates rapidly,
But cannot pause
Before the last great mounting spring…   25
And now, as she strikes,
Her front rears up agonisingly…

A crunch of severed muscle,
Twisted sinew and seared flesh,
A splendid face ripped out of recognition.   30
And I wonder, with my dying breath,
That this superb machine was built for death.

D.J Brindley

1   What machine is the jaguar being compared to in the poem?

_____

2 Who is attacked in the poem? Give a line from the poem to back up your answer.

_____

_____

3 What type of person is the jaguar compared to in the second stanza?

_____

4 What is meant by the sentence 'And now, as she strikes'?

_____

_____

5 What is happening when 'Suddenly the light thins sharply'?

_____

_____

6 In your own words describe what happens in the last two stanzas.

_____

_____

_____

_____

_____

Section 1b: Written text

The Big Time

I guess that I became a representative player because I didn't have the sense to get out of Norman Kernahern's way. It was in the trials and I was in the Possibles against the Probables who had jerseys all the same colour and so we reckoned they were first picks. Norman was a sort of local Goliath who was in the special class at Rennick and like most in that class he was a bit older, and different. He had very hairy legs and few words. When he was given the ball and the line pointed out to him, he used to put his head down and go for it like a jersey bull. None of us in the other school teams liked to play against him because he seemed to have a strange disregard for pain – his own, or any that he might inflict.

I was what was called a breakaway, which meant that like a lot of other kids I was somewhat betwixt and between as far as speed and size went. Anyway, to be picked for both trial games was really something for me, although I didn't let on. My father was pleased when I told him. Good on you, he said. You can make the big time if you get stuck in. Who knows. I imagined what it would be like to come home and tell him that I had been selected for the under fourteens as my brother had.

So twice I did the foolish thing and tackled Normie from the front. The usual thing was to let him go bullocking past and then try to drag him down by weight of numbers from behind. The first time I went low all right and he went down with a wallop; the second time I got one of his great mud-caked knees fair in the face, but at least the impact jarred the ball loose from his arms and he wasn't able to run on and score. The blood ran steadily from my nose and vividly polka-dotted the winter mud; my front teeth squelched a little in their gums when I tried them between my fingers. But I heard Mr Ellenor saying to the other selector that they certainly needed tacklers, and that my brother had been a bloody good age group player. So I pretended that I wanted to get back on to see out the last fifteen minutes or so, which was certainly a lie.

The Big Time, Owen Marshall.

1 Give an adjective used to describe Norman. _____

2 Norman was concerned about getting hurt: a: True b: False

3 The narrator is very large and very fast: a: True b: False

4 Give two examples of *colloquial* language that give this extract a conversational tone.

_____

_____

5 'Squelched' (line 20) is an example of:

a: Adverb   b: Epistle   c: Simile   d: Onomatopoeia

6 Write an example of a simile from the extract. _____

_____

7 Explain, using examples and quotations from the text, what we learn about the narrator of this extract.

_____

_____

_____

8 Explain, using examples and quotations from the text, what we learn about Norman in this extract.

_____

_____

_____

_____

Section 1c: Visual text

1 In the cartoon, 'jacked up' means:

a: Raised   b: Applauded   c: Written to   d: Organised

2 What is the event or issue that inspired the cartoon? _____

_____

3 Give an example of slang from the cartoon. _____

_____

4 Identify the pun in the cartoon. _____

_____

5 Explain how verbal and visual features combine to create a stereotype of Maori radicals.

_____

_____

_____

_____

ISBN 9780170195959

You must write an essay from **TWO of the following three sections** (2a, 2b and 2c). You must write **at least 300 words** for each essay. Ensure you include as many **details and quotations** from the text as you can.

Section 2a: Show understanding of an extended written text

Choose **ONE** of the following questions and answer using an extended text (novel, drama, non-fiction) you have studied in class this year.

1 Describe an important moment in a text you have studied in class and explain why it is important.

2 Describe a main character in a text you have studied this year and explain the importance of that character on the text as a whole.

3 Explain an important idea in your text and explain, with detailed reasons, why it was relevant to you.

4 Describe a major conflict in your text, how it was resolved, and explain, with detailed reasons, why this conflict was important.

Section 2b: Show understanding of short written text

Choose **ONE** of the following questions and answer using **TWO** short written text (poetry, short stories etc) you have studied in class this year.

1 Explain, with detail how three interesting language techniques (metaphor, alliteration, personification etc) were used to make your text effective.

2 Describe a main character in each text. Explain what you learnt from the words and/or actions of this character.

3 Explain an important idea in your text and explain, with detailed reasons, why it was relevant to you.

4 Describe two important images in your text and explain, with detailed reasons, why each is important.

Section 2c: Show understanding of short visual text

Choose **ONE** of the following questions and answer using a visual text you have studied in class this year.

1 Describe how sound effects and music were effectively used to help create the mood of one scene from your text.

2 Describe how the director used film techniques to convey the main idea/s in your text.

3 Describe a turning point in your text and explain, with detailed reasons, why this is important.

4 Explain an important event in your text and explain why it was an important event.

Write a formal essay on **ONE** of the following topics. You can write **for, or against**, the topic you choose. **Plan** your essay. **Support** your points with **examples and explanations**. Write approximately **300 words**.

1 Sport rules New Zealand.

2 Only people can make people happy.

3 The best learning occurs outside the classroom.

4 Young people are slaves to technology.

5 Our environment must be looked after.

6 Students benefit from experiencing an overseas exchange.

You could always write all of the above essays if you need some extra study activities.

ISBN 9780170195959

Use the following pages to help keep your work in one place. We suggest you use refill for any planning and drafting, and use this space for your final product. Don't forget to date and reference the appropriate unit and page number.

ISBN 9780170195959

Use the following pages to help keep your work in one place. We suggest you use refill for any planning and drafting, and use this space for your final product. Don't forget to date and reference the appropriate unit and page number.

ISBN 9780170195959

Use the following pages to help keep your work in one place. We suggest you use refill for any planning and drafting, and use this space for your final product. Don't forget to date and reference the appropriate unit and page number.

ISBN 9780170195959

Use the following pages to help keep your work in one place. We suggest you use refill for any planning and drafting, and use this space for your final product. Don't forget to date and reference the appropriate unit and page number.

ISBN 9780170195959

Use the following pages to help keep your work in one place. We suggest you use refill for any planning and drafting, and use this space for your final product. Don't forget to date and reference the appropriate unit and page number.

ISBN 9780170195959

Use the following pages to help keep your work in one place. We suggest you use refill for any planning and drafting, and use this space for your final product. Don't forget to date and reference the appropriate unit and page number.

ISBN 9780170195959

Use the following pages to help keep your work in one place. We suggest you use refill for any planning and drafting, and use this space for your final product. Don't forget to date and reference the appropriate unit and page number.

ISBN 9780170195959

ISBN 9780170195959

Use the following pages to help keep your work in one place. We suggest you use refill for any planning and drafting, and use this space for your final product. Don't forget to date and reference the appropriate unit and page number.

ISBN 9780170195959

Use the following pages to help keep your work in one place. We suggest you use refill for any planning and drafting, and use this space for your final product. Don't forget to date and reference the appropriate unit and page number.

ISBN 9780170195959

Use the following pages to help keep your work in one place. We suggest you use refill for any planning and drafting, and use this space for your final product. Don't forget to date and reference the appropriate unit and page number.

ISBN 9780170195959

ISBN 9780170195959

Use the following pages to help keep your work in one place. We suggest you use refill for any planning and drafting, and use this space for your final product. Don't forget to date and reference the appropriate unit and page number.

ISBN 9780170195959